T0361228

ROUTLEDGE LIBRARY EDITIONS: HUMAN RESOURCE MANAGEMENT

Volume 19

EMPLOYEE RELATIONS AUDITS

EMPLOYEE RELATIONS AUDITS

C. JENNINGS, W.E.J. MCCARTHY
AND R. UNDY

Routledge
Taylor & Francis Group

LONDON AND NEW YORK

First published in 1990 by Routledge

This edition first published in 2017
by Routledge
2 Park Square, Milton Park, Abingdon, Oxon OX14 4RN

and by Routledge
711 Third Avenue, New York, NY 10017

Routledge is an imprint of the Taylor & Francis Group, an informa business

© 1990 HMSO

British Library Cataloguing in Publication Data
A catalogue record for this book is available from the British Library

ISBN: 978-1-138-80870-6 (Set)
ISBN: 978-1-315-18006-9 (Set) (ebk)
ISBN: 978-0-415-78658-4 (Volume 19) (hbk)
ISBN: 978-1-315-22693-4 (Volume 19) (ebk)

Publisher's Note
The publisher has gone to great lengths to ensure the quality of this reprint but points out that some imperfections in the original copies may be apparent.

Disclaimer
The publisher has made every effort to trace copyright holders and would welcome correspondence from those they have been unable to trace.

Employee relations audits

C. Jennings, W.E.J. McCarthy and
R. Undy

London and New York

First published 1990
by Routledge
11 New Fetter Lane, London EC4P 4EE

Simultaneously published in the USA and Canada
by Routledge
a division of Routledge, Chapman and Hall, Inc.
29 West 35th Street, New York, NY 10001

Phototypeset in 10pt Times and Optima by
Mews Photosetting, Beckenham, Kent
Printed and bound in Great Britain by
Biddles Ltd, Guildford and King's Lynn

British Library Cataloguing in Publication Data

Jennings, C.
    Employee relations audits.
    1. Great Britain. Companies. Auditing
    I. Title II. McCarthy, W.E.J. III. Undy, Roger
    657′.45′0941

    ISBN 0-415-03635-6

Library of Congress Cataloging-in-Publication Data

Jennings, C., 1942–
    Employee relations audits / by C. Jennings, W.E.J. McCarthy, R.
    Undy.
        p.   cm.
    Simultaneously published in the USA and Canada – T.p. verso.
    ISBN 0-415-03635-6
    1. Personnel management – United States – Auditing. 2. Industrial
    relations – United States – Auditing. I. McCarthy, W.E.J. (William
    Edward John) II. Undy, R. (Roger) III. Title.
    HF5549.2.U5J46   1990
    658.3′15–dc20   89-10505
                                                              CIP

Contents

Preface

In 1983 the Manpower Services Commission published a manual entitled *Managers and Industrial Relations: the Identification of Training Needs*. This was the outcome of five years' research which we conducted at Templeton College, the Oxford Centre for Management Studies. As the title suggests, the intention was that the manual should be used for identifying line managers' industrial relations (IR) training needs. Data were collected by self-completion questionnaires and analysed by computer and the approach became known as the management IR training audit.

In the course of this earlier research it became evident that many personnel managers were more interested in analysing employee relations in general, than they were in identifying their colleagues' IR training needs. In particular they saw advantages in converting the training audit into a tool which could show what was actually happening in employee relations on the shop-floor or in the office as perceived by line management. This was seen as an essential first step prior to intervening to effect improvements. Some managers also expressed interest in an audit which could be applied to relatively small groups of managers and employees and the resulting data analysed without necessarily having to process it by computer.

The widespread interest we encountered in auditing employee relations in general led to further research and development work and this book is the result. We have simplified the audit process without reducing its proven effectiveness in both large and small employing units. The original questionnaire material has been revised and greatly expanded for use with managers, blue-collar, and white-collar employees. This broadening of the audit to encompass shop-floor views has been found to enhance greatly the value of the data collected.

During the development of the audit approach we found that the interests of many managers had shifted away from traditional industrial relations issues, where management–trade union relationships were of central importance, to focus more on manager–employee relations. In recognition of this change we have developed questions which are more appropriate for analysing the direct relationship between managers and their employees. As will be seen these questions supplement those which address managers' relationships with employee representatives.

The local Government Training Board (LGTB) and the Advisory Conciliation and Arbitration Service (ACAS)* worked closely with us in the development of this audit. They were involved in piloting the audit material and helped test it across a wide range of small and large organizations in the public and private sectors. We are therefore indebted to the LGTB and ACAS for their assistance and to the Manpower Services Commission for funding the research. However, any errors or omissions are the responsibility of the authors.

Sid Jennings
Bill McCarthy
Roger Undy

*The LGTB has published *Improving Local Government Employee Relations – How are you Managing?* which covers similar aspects of employee relations as this manual but is tailored to potential users in local government. Organizations seeking an independent body to examine their internal employee relations can approach ACAS for assistance. ACAS is experienced in using questionnaires for IR audits and expects employees and/or their representatives to be involved in the exercise.

Introduction

In recent years auditing techniques have increasingly been applied in areas of business activity outside the direct concern of accountants. The audit process can be seen as a means of collecting information on the particular activity of interest in order to identify the current situation within the organization concerned. Thus for an employee relations (ER) audit, information is collected on the current behaviour and attitudes of managers, supervisors, and, where relevant, employees and these are then evaluated against the requirements of policies, procedures, and, in some instances, legislation. For example, an audit in the area of equal opportunities would involve gathering information on the way in which employees are recruited and selected for promotion and training. This would then be compared with the requirements of the internal policy (if this exists) and legislation on race and sex discrimination. If a gap is found between the behaviour identified by the audit and that prescribed as desirable by policy or the law, then suitable initiatives can be taken to bring these into line.

It is the emphasis on identifying current behaviour in some particular aspect of employee relations covered by policy or legislation which differentiates an ER audit from an employee attitude survey. Hence, this manual is not intended to provide the means of measuring job satisfaction *per se*, but to provide valuable first-hand feedback on the effectiveness of ER policies and procedures as well as giving an insight into the knowledge and attitudes of those who are expected to implement them.

This publication has specifically been developed as a 'self-help' or 'do-it-yourself' manual for organizations seeking to audit some aspect of employee relations. As a potential user of the manual you will need to know (i) what aspects of employee relations can be audited, (ii) who should participate, (iii) the resources required, and (iv) the potential benefits. Each of these will be examined in turn before discussing how the manual should be applied.

1

Employee relations audits

(i) Aspects of employee relations that can be audited

Organizations are likely to have widely differing views as to the scope of employee relations. A narrow perspective of employee relations could limit it to management–trade union relationships, whereas a broader perspective could include things like management style, leadership, employee motivation, and job satisfaction. As the authors believe that it should be possible to evaluate the information collected in an audit against some reasonably acceptable criteria, they have concentrated on those areas of employee relations where policies and procedures most frequently exist. In practice, organizations have expressed most interest in auditing five key areas:

- communication and consultation
- health and safety at work
- equality of opportunity
- trade union representation and employee grievances
- disciplinary matters

This manual provides you with comprehensive questionnaire material and detailed guidance in implementing an employee relations audit in each of the above areas. If you would like to cover other aspects of employee relations then you will still be able to apply the methodology of the manual but you will have to develop your own questionnaire material from the guidelines supplied.

(ii) Participants in an audit

Information for an audit is supplied by means of self-completion questionnaires which can be completed by managers, supervisors, and employees. The whole of your organization can be audited or particular sites (or even departments) can provide the focus. Whereas there is probably a minimum number of participants, e.g. fifty, required to make your audit viable, there appears to be no upper limit apart from that determined by available resources. It has been found that there can be wide differences in the perception of managers, supervisors, and employees with respect to what is happening in the same employee relations activity. Experience clearly indicates that a more comprehensive picture is obtained of what is actually happening if all interest groups are included in the audit.

(iii) Resources required for an audit

The method which this manual employs has been developed to minimize the resources needed for its successful application. This was done to enable the audit to be applied by relatively small organizations. Although it is expected that most users of the manual are likely to be personnel specialists, this is not an essential requirement. If you follow the method described in this manual you could complete an audit utilizing a single questionnaire in six weeks and in this period you could expect to spend approximately one-half of your time on the exercise. Obviously a very large audit requiring the development of two separate questionnaires for use with managers and employees on several sites will be more time-consuming. Apart from the time you spend administering the audit and the time participants spend in completing questionnaires, other costs can be quite low. There will be printing and possibly postage costs if questionnaires are returned by this means. Manual methods of data analysis or the use of in-house computing facilities will minimize the costs of processing the information from completed questionnaires.

(iv) The potential benefits of an audit

If you follow the guidelines of this manual, your audit will provide you with valuable information with respect to the particular area of employee relations you have chosen, including a 'snap-shot' of current practice. The effectiveness of your existing policies and procedures can then be assessed by comparing and contrasting the behaviour and attitudes these were intended to produce with those revealed by the audit. Similarly, if there are thought to be problems in particular areas, for example, in communications between supervisors and employees, the perceptions of both groups can be identified and used for prescribing remedial action. Information of this kind can also be used for determining training needs and, if you have provided training in the past, for obtaining feedback on its effectiveness. The information collected can be analysed in aggregate form or disaggregated by reference to site, department, function, age, or other criteria. In many cases the latter form of analysis will enable you to target policy and other initiatives at those parts of the organization or groups where they are needed most.

Using the manual

There are two parts to the manual.

Part one outlines the seven stages in the audit process and each is explained in some detail. You will need to understand fully each of these stages to implement an audit successfully and, as these are interrelated, you must familiarize yourself with all of them at the outset. This will help in planning your audit.

Part two contains a comprehensive set of reference material for auditing five different aspects of employee relations. If you have already

3

decided upon the focus of your audit then you will only need to consult the relevant section. However, if you are undecided you should consult each section and choose that subject which is of most interest to you. There is a validated set of questions for each audit which you can use to construct your questionnaire(s). You will note that Audits 1, 2, and 3 contain questions for use with managers and employees whereas Audits 4 and 5 only contain questions for managers. Questions recommended for managers are coded MQ and those for employees EQ. In addition, there are hints on possible audit objectives; the selection of participants; the selection and the modification of model questions; and the analysis of findings.

You will find that if you select the reference material for one of the audits in Part two and follow the stages in the audit process outlined in Part one, you should be able to implement successfully an employee relations audit.

Part one

Stages in the audit process

Stages in the audit process

This section explains the various stages in implementing an employee relations audit. You should read this section carefully before starting your audit in order to understand fully the various elements in an audit and to plan for them. There are seven stages to consider:

Stage 1: decide which aspect of ER is to be audited and specify your objectives;
Stage 2: decide who is to participate;
Stage 3: develop the questionnaire;
Stage 4: refine and test the questionnaire;
Stage 5: brief participants and distribute the questionnaires;
Stage 6: summarize information from completed questionnaires;
Stage 7: analyse the findings and draw up recommendations.

It is very important that you follow each stage rigorously; avoid the temptation to cut corners, otherwise you are likely to fail to achieve your objectives.

Stage 1: decide which aspect of ER is to be audited and specify your objectives

At the outset you will have to decide which aspect of employee relations is to be the focus of your audit. This manual contains reference material for the following:

- communication and consultation (Audit 1)
- health and safety at work (Audit 2)
- equality of opportunity (Audit 3)
- trade union representation and employee grievances (Audit 4)
- disciplinary matters (Audit 5)

If you decide to audit some aspect of employee relations not listed above, then you will have to develop your own questionnaire material. However, the method outlined in this section will still be valid.

Once you have decided what is to be audited, you will then need to specify your objectives. It is likely that you will be seeking sensitive information from participants and you will also raise expectations concerning action over the findings. Hence, it is very important that you think through carefully what you are setting out to achieve in your audit. Your objectives should not only have a direct influence on the content of your questionnaire(s) but should also assist in 'selling' the audit to those whose co-operation you need for it to be a success.

In practice, objectives can relate to the identification of problems, the effectiveness of current policies, attitudes, or training needs. Examples of audit objectives are included with each set of questions.

Note: Clearly defined objectives are essential to give direction to an ER audit.

Stage 2: decide who is to participate

At this stage there are two key questions to be tackled: Who is to complete a questionnaire? and Who is to be consulted? Each of these will be considered in turn.

Who is to complete a questionnaire?

This decision is likely to be influenced by your audit objectives. For example, if you are seeking to evaluate the effectiveness of your channels of management-employee communications, then clearly members of management and employees would both have to supply information if an accurate evaluation is to be carried out. On the other hand, if your prime objective is to determine management training needs in the handling of disciplinary matters, then it may be that managers and supervisors alone should complete questionnaires. It is important to note that if you decide that managers and employees will be asked to complete questionnaires, then you should be prepared to develop two separate questionnaires. Attempts to develop a single questionnaire for these two groups will result in key management and employee questions being omitted and create problems in the wording of questions that are included.

Once it has been decided whether managers and/or employees are to complete questionnaires then it will be necessary to decide whether all members of the relevant groups will participate or whether sampling will be used. Although it may not be difficult to determine a sample size which will produce statistically sound findings, there are strong arguments for 100 per cent coverage within the relevant groups. If, for example, a 33 per cent sample is used in a communications audit it will be necessary to explain to individuals why they have been included or excluded. Also, if the findings are not very palatable to some members of senior management, they might be tempted to discredit them by stressing that the findings are only representative of the views of a minority. Further, it will prove particularly valuable, when seeking commitment to implement changes arising from the audit, to have previously involved all those affected by the changes in the audit, hence giving them ownership of the findings.

However, it is acknowledged that for large organizations it may be necessary to reduce the number of those completing questionnaires to manageable proportions. If sampling cannot be avoided then an across-the-board percentage sample is not necessarily the best way of proceeding. One alternative approach which has been successfully applied in the past is to select three or four representative departments (or sites) from within the organization and have 100 per cent coverage in these departments (sites). A second alternative approach is to permit all parts of the organization to participate but to weight the samples differently. For example, 20 per cent of supervisors and 100 per cent of middle and senior managers could participate.

If you do decide to use sampling techniques then you are advised to consult *Employment and Manpower Surveys – A Practitioner's Guide* by D. Parsons. This provides sensible advice on sampling in general and on the selection of an appropriate sample frame.

Who is to be consulted?

There are likely to be a number of individuals and groups within your organization who can influence the success or failure of your audit. It will be necessary to identify these key people and to develop a strategy for winning their support. This can be done by involving them at various stages in the development and administration of the questionnaire. Particular groups can be involved as follows:

(a) *Personnel department:* If you are a personnel specialist you are advised to seek the support of your colleagues, especially if the questionnaire covers some aspect of employee relations of particular interest to them. An audit exercise could easily be put in jeopardy if it does not have unequivocal support from within your own department. At the very least, key members of the personnel department should be asked to comment on a draft of the questionnaire and their comments should be seen to have been given some weight. Consideration might also be given to involving one or more of your colleagues in the analysis of your findings (i.e. at Stage 7).

(b) *Senior line managers:* If you want your audit to have credibility within the departments which are to participate, then it is crucial to 'sell' it to the senior managers concerned. This can be done by asking them to examine the wording of the draft questionnaire to ensure it is relevant for their department. You can also ask them to nominate one or two individuals to participate in the testing of the questionnaire (Stage 4). Finally, you can offer to provide them with detailed summaries of all responses from their own department. Experience has shown that senior management is not slow in recognizing the potential benefits of the information sought by an audit and in this respect a well thought out questionnaire often 'sells' itself.

(c) *Trade union representatives:* If you are using a questionnaire in a unionized organization, but issuing it solely to members of management, it may help prevent concern arising on the shop-floor about its purpose, if trade unions representing manual and white-collar employees are informed of your intentions at the start of the exercise via the normal consultative machinery. If your managers themselves are unionized then a more detailed consultation with their representatives may be required. This could involve permitting the union to examine the questionnaire and supplying it with a summary of the audit findings and recommendations. It can also be of value to invite one or more of the management trade union representatives to participate in the testing of the questionnaire (Stage 4).

If you intend asking unionized employees to complete a questionnaire then their trade union representative may be expected to seek a direct involvement in its design and administration. In these circumstances the involvement of the union could vary from minor consultation over its purpose to full participation in its design and administration via a management–union working party. If the union is closely involved in the early stages then you could find it valuable to involve them in the analysis and share with them the audit findings. It should be borne in mind that given the sensitivity attached to some of the issues raised, attempts to question unionized employees without union involvement may well be counter-productive.

Note: The greater the number participating in your audit, the greater will be the credibility of your findings. Also, the more consultation that takes place, the greater will be the commitment to act upon the findings.

Stage 3: develop the questionnaire

Once you have set your objectives and decided on your target population, you can now begin to develop the questionnaire(s). The basic principles for designing a questionnaire from the model questions contained in this manual are the same regardless of the subject area.

They also apply to the development of both management and employee questionnaires and are as follows:

Select no more than three or four background information questions

The model questions in each area of employee relations covered contain a number of background information questions which are used to determine a respondent's job grade, department, age, etc. In the analysis of your findings, each of these characteristics could prove significant in explaining differences in responses received. At the outset you will not know which are going to prove most valuable, therefore it might be tempting to include all of the relevant background information questions. Unfortunately, the more background questions you ask, the more the confidentiality of respondents is eroded and this can have an adverse effect upon the quality of answers provided and the response rate achieved. It is because of these considerations that you are advised to include no more than three or four background questions in your questionnaire. Guidance is provided on which of these questions have proved most useful in the past.

Consult model questions and select those which will assist in the achievement of objectives.

All of the model questions can provide useful information and you might consider retaining nearly all of them. This should be avoided! Retain only those questions which are relevant to your objectives and discard the remainder. To assist you in the selection of questions, those which have proven particularly useful in the past have been marked with an asterisk, e.g. MQ4*.

You will note that some questions seek very similar information. Avoid the retention of questions which duplicate the information sought. Also in some sections there are a high proportion of knowledge questions on policies, procedures, the law, etc. If to achieve your objectives you need to evaluate the level of understanding of these items then some questions of this kind are clearly relevant. However, do not retain too many knowledge questions, otherwise, respondents will perceive the questionnaire as a 'test'.

Modify the wording of all retained questions

Examine your retained questions and ensure that they comply with your current policies and procedures and that their wording is compatible with your own internal terminology. Where 'the organization' is used, replace this with something more appropriate, e.g. the actual name of your organization. For some questions you might ask respondents to provide additional information by including instructions such as:

If you have answered NO to the above question please explain why:

....

....

Written comments can be very useful but unfortunately they can represent difficulties at the analysis stage. Also, if too many written comments are requested, this can have an adverse effect on the response rate. It is therefore recommended that the number of questions requiring written answers will be limited and, as a rule of thumb, no more than four or five be included in the finalized questionnaire.

Develop additional questions using numeric coding

It is to be expected that you will want to develop additional questions to those provided in this manual. This should pose no problem as long as the format of the model question is followed, i.e. numbers are used to code answers:

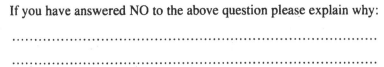

Yes	*No*	*Not sure*
1	2	3

Numeric coding greatly simplifies the summarizing and analysis of responses whether this is done manually or by computer. Care should be taken in deciding the place in the draft questionnaire to slot any additional questions you develop.

Put your questions in logical order

It is of assistance to those completing a questionnaire if the questions are asked in a logical sequence. A quick method for ordering those questions you decide to use involves writing each one of them in pencil on a separate reference card. It is relatively straightforward then to place the set of reference cards in a logical order. The questions can be checked for consistency in wording at the same time.

Assemble a draft questionnaire

To convert your selected questions into a self-completion questionnaire it will be necessary to include an 'Introduction' page, an 'Instructions for answering questionnaire' page, and a 'Completed questionnaires' page.
    The 'Introduction' page should explain the objectives of the audit,

confidentiality aspects, the need for maximum co-operation, and how the information will be used. It has proven useful in the past to have the message on this page signed by a senior executive.

The 'Instructions for answering questionnaire' page explains to participants how the questionnaire should be completed.

The 'Completed questionnaires' page should ask respondents to check that all relevant questions have been answered; give directions on what to do with completed questionnaires; and thank participants for their co-operation.

Note: Your questionnaire should be relatively straightforward to understand and complete. It should not contain superfluous questions or create unnecessary problems at the analysis stage.

Stage 4: refine and test the questionnaire

Refining the draft questionnaire

It is likely that your draft questionnaire can be improved by inviting key individuals within your organization to comment upon it. Hence, personnel specialists, line managers, and, where appropriate, trade union representatives sould be consulted on the wording of the questionnaire and, in particular, be asked to identify any obvious gaps in its coverage. As a result, certain questions might be re-worded and additional ones developed. Experience has shown that widespread consultation at this stage is likely to be repaid by a much higher degree of commitment to the audit.

Testing the questionnaire

Once you are reasonably satisfied with the draft questionnaire, it will be necessary to test it with a small group (e.g. six or eight persons) representing a cross-section of those who will participate in the audit proper. The objective in testing the questionnaire is to establish whether questions are unambiguous and completion instructions easy to follow.

The test group should meet together and be briefed on the audit exercise. They should then be issued with a draft questionnaire and asked to complete it there and then. Whilst completing the questionnaire members of the group should note:

- questions they do not fully understand;
- questions where the meaning is not immediately clear;
- questions where none of the answers listed is appropriate; and
- any other difficulties encountered.

Once the whole group has finished completing the questionnaire, you should go through each question in turn and note the comments of the group. If members of the test group are agreeable the completed questionnaires should be collected and examined later to ensure that procedural instructions were followed in the required manner.

Once the comments of the test group have been evaluated, you will be in a position to finalize and print the questionnaire.

Note: The status of the questionnaire, as perceived by those expected to complete it, will be greatly enhanced if it is well laid out, printed to a high standard, and bound in suitable covers.

Stage 5: brief participants and distribute questionnaires

This stage is crucial if a high response rate is to be achieved. All those expected to complete a questionnaire should be given the opportunity of attending a briefing session and approximately 30 minutes should be allowed for each session.

Briefing of participants

You are the best person to brief the participants, and you can do this by addressing them directly in groups. Experience has shown that the size of the briefing group does not affect, to any great extent, the response rate achieved. At the briefing participants should be informed of the following:

- objectives of the audit
- who will participate
- how the audit is to be conducted
- the advantages of participating
- confidentiality of responses
- feedback of findings
- completion procedure
- what to do with completed questionnaires

After the briefing participants should be allowed to ask questions and it is important that they are given honest answers. In some organizations it might be appropriate to ask participants to complete their questionnaires at the briefing session. In this instance, response rates approaching 100 per cent can be achieved. If this method is considered inappropriate then participants should be asked to take away their questionnaire, complete it, and return it to some stated internal collection point within a set period of time, e.g. two or three days. Avoid giving too long a period for completion because participants are likely to put their questionnaires to one side and forget about them. A reminder can be sent to all participants after the set period has elapsed so as to jog the memories of those who have forgotten. With this second method of completion, response rates in excess of 80 per cent can still be expected from managers and supervisors and over 65 per cent for other employees.

Note: Briefing facilitates the achievement of high response rate and the development of interest and commitment.

Stage 6: summarize information from completed questionnaires

The information provided by respondents will have to be summarized before it can be analysed and this can be done manually or by computer. As a rule of thumb, a questionnaire containing up to forty questions takes about 5 minutes to summarize manually by the method outlined below. If your questionnaire is significantly longer than this, and/or a very large number of completed questionnaires have to be processed, you might choose to use computing facilities.

Summarizing information manually

This involves five steps:

1. Sort the completed questionnaires in a logical order, based on factors you intend to use in your analysis. For example, the questionnaires can initially be sorted according to department and then be sorted according to job grade within each department.

2. Write on each of the sorted questionnaires an individual reference number. Thus, if you have 128 completed questionnaires, then your numbering will be 1, 2, 3 . . . 128. This will prove useful in the analysis if you have need to verify that a particular response to a question has been recorded correctly.

3. Make out a summary sheet. This is demonstrated by reference to an extract from an employee communications questionnaire that was used within a region of a public utility organization (see Questionnaire Extract). The column headings of a summary sheet for the employee communications questionnaire would be as follows:

Ref. no.	*Q1* (6)	*Q2* (3)	*Q3* (3)	*Q4.1* (2)	*Q4.2* (2)	*Q4.3* (2)	*Q5* (7)	*Q6* (3)	*Q7* (2)	*Q8* (2)

The column headed 'Ref. no.' refers to the individual reference given to each questionnaire (see above). The figure in brackets below each question number, e.g. the (3) below Q2, indicates the maximum value for a legitimate answer to this particular question. In this case

15

the only possible correct answers to Q2 are:

Monthly staff grade	1
Senior officer grade	2
Higher manager grade	3

Similarly, the (7) below Q5 indicates that there are seven possible correct answers. Q4 is allocated three columns, i.e. Q4.1–Q4.3. This is because there are three parts to this question and each requires a separate answer.

Table 1 Sample summary sheet

Ref. no.	Q1 (6)	Q2 (3)	Q3 (3)	Q4.1 (2)	Q4.2 (2)	Q4.3 (2)	Q5 (7)	Q6 (3)	Q7 (2)	Q8 (2)
1	Mark.	3	3	1	1	2	1	1	1	1
2	Mark.	3	3	1	1	2	1	2	2	2
3	Mark.	3	1	2	1	1	2	2	2	2
4	Mark.	2	1	2	1	2	2	1	2	1
5	Mark.	2	3	1	3	1	4	3	2	2
6	Mark.	2	3	3	1	2	5	2	2	2
7	Mark.	2	3	1	2	2	5	2	2	2
8	Mark.	2	1	2	3	2	4	1	2	1
9	Mark.	2	3	2	1	2	5	1	1	1
10	Mark.	1	2	1	1	0	1	1	1	2
11	Mark.	1	2	3	2	2	1	1	1	1
12	Mark.	1	3	1	2	1	2	2	2	1
13	Mark.	1	3	1	1	1	1	1	2	1
14	Eng.	3	1	3	2	1	3	1	2	2
15	Eng.	3	3	1	1	2	3	1	2	1
16	Eng.	3	3	3	1	2	5	0	1	1
17	Eng.	3	2	1	1	2	4	1	2	1
18	Eng.	2	3	2	2	1	1	3	2	1
19	Eng.	2	2	4	2	2	4	1	1	2
20	Eng.	2	3	0	1	2	1	2	2	1
21	Eng.	2	3	2	2	2	1	1	1	1
22	Eng.	2	1	2	1	2	5	1	2	2
23	Eng.	2	2	2	1	1	5	1	2	1
24	Eng.	2	1	1	2	1	4	1	1	1
25	Eng.	2	3	1	2	2	3	2	1	2
26	Eng.	2	1	3	2	1	1	1	1	2
27	Eng.	2	3	1	1	0	2	1	1	1
28	Eng.	2	3	1	2	1	1	0	1	2
29	Eng.	2	3	2	2	2	1	2	1	1
30	Eng.	2	2	2	2	2	1	2	2	1

(0 – no answer given)

Note: From Table 1, it can be seen that the questionnaire with the reference number 4 was completed by a senior officer in the marketing department, and whose answers to Q3, Q4.1, and Q4.2 are coded 1, 2, and 1, respectively. Reference to the questionnaire can quickly provide the actual questions asked and the meaning of the coded answers.

4. Record on the summary sheet the relevant information from each completed questionnaire. This involves taking each questionnaire in turn and recording the reference number, the department and grade of the respondent (and/or other relevant background information) and his/her coded answers for each question. A completed summary sheet would appear as shown in Table 1.

5. Ensure that all answers coded on the summary sheet are valid. This is done by checking down the columns of your summary sheet to ensure that no value has been recorded which is higher than the highest possible value for each answer, i.e. must not exceed the figure in brackets at the top of the column. With reference to Table 1, it can be seen that for the questionnaire with the reference number 19, a value of 4 has been recorded for Q4.1. However, the maximum value of any answer to this question is 3. Hence, an error must have been made in transferring information from the questionnaire on to the summary sheet. It will be necessary to refer back to Q4.1 in the questionnaire numbered 19 and correct the error.

Once all information has been transferred to the summary sheet and errors in recording corrected, you will then be in a position to start analysis of your findings.

Using a computer to summarize findings

If you have a large number of questionnaires to process, it is sensible to make use of computing facilities. You can utilize in-house facilities or an external agency. An IBM PC/XT or IBM PC/AT or compatible machine using hard discs will prove ideal. There is a wide range of survey software packages available for these machines, e.g. SPSS, P Stat, SAS, which will enable you to carry out quite sophisticated analysis. Even if you only have access to a basic IBM PC or compatible machine using floppy discs, then a survey package such as SNAP is available with which you can carry out a limited range of data analysis including cross-tabulations. Whether you purchase one of these ready-made packages, develop your own software, or hire an agency to do the computing for you, there are a number of basic steps which should be followed. These are:

(a) ensure that the final draft of the questionnaire is suitable for processing by computer;
(b) allocate an identification number to each completed questionnaire;
(c) pre-edit all questionnaires, i.e. check that the correct completion procedure has been followed and code errors and questions not answered;
(d) transfer data from the questionnaires on to the computer file;

(e) correct any coding or punching errors in the computer file; and
(f) summarize findings according to department, grade, etc. in the form of tables (see Stage 7).

Note: This stage involves the straightforward processing of questionnaire data. If you are using manual methods, then you can enlist clerical support for the routine transfer of information on to summary sheets. If you are using computing facilities, then data processing staff can be utilized.

Stage 7: analyse the findings and draw up recommendations

Once all the information has been transferred on to summary sheets or a computer file, analysis can be started.

A relatively quick method of identifying the most significant findings is to use a fluorescent marker with the summary sheet. For example, with reference to the Questionnaire Extract on pages 20–1, the wording of Q7 was:

Have your responsibilities for the communication of information to employees been explained to you (i.e. what information should be given and who should receive it)?

Yes No
  1   2

If you are particularly interested in those respondents who answer 'No', then you can look down the Q7 column and mark all of the 2s with your fluorescent marker. From the total number of respondents giving these answers you can decide whether a widespread problem is indicated. Also, by checking whether these 'No' answers are clustered in particular departments, or job grades, you can decide whether localized problems are indicated. With a summary sheet (or suitable computer package) you can easily use the responses to one question to analyse responses to other questions. Hence for the example above, you could extract the sub-group of respondents who had indicated that they had not been informed of their responsibilities for communicating information, and compare their answers to other questions against those of all other respondents.

A more systematic method of analysis is to make tables with number of responses and percentages for each question based on department and grade. For example, the answers to Q7 could be presented as:

(a) Department

	Yes	*No*
Marketing	17(61%)	11(39%)
Finance	11(52%)	10(48%)
Engineering	14(38%)	23(62%)

	Yes	No
Management services	22(73%)	8(27%)
Personnel	7(78%)	2(22%)
Supplies and transport	10(37%)	17(63%)
	81(53%)	71(47%)

(b) Grade

	Yes	No
Monthly staff	35(41%)	51(59%)
Senior officers	28(65%)	15(35%)
Higher managers	18(78%)	5(22%)
	81(53%)	71(47%)

Tables such as these can easily be assembled from summary sheets, and there are computer packages that present data in this manner.

When analysing the responses to each question you will have to decide how significant they are and whether action is to be taken as a result. In the tabulated answers to Q7 in the example above, you will note that 47 per cent of respondents maintained that they had not been informed of their responsibilities for information to employees. If your audit results revealed a similar situation, then you would have to decide whether this situation is acceptable. If you conclude that it is not, then you will have to select appropriate initiatives to bring about the required changes.

Your initial audit objectives will clearly have a major influence on what you are looking for in your analysis. However, experience has shown that very important findings can emerge which were completely unexpected at the outset. Hence, if you wish to gain the maximum benefit from your audit it might be necessary to look beyond your narrow audit objectives at the analysis stage.

Once you have identified those areas requiring action you should be in a position to put forward recommendations.

Note: It is often advantageous to encourage certain groups to analyse their own data, as this can promote greater commitment to achieving desirable improvements.

Questionnaire Extract

Employee communications

1. To which of the following functions does your job belong?

Marketing	1
Finance	2
Engineering	3
Management services	4
Personnel	5
Supplies and transport	6

2. In which of the following grades is your job?

Monthly staff grade	1
Senior officer grade	2
Higher manager grade	3

3. How many years of service have you had in a management/ supervisory position with the region?

Less than 2 years	1
2-10 years	2
Over 10 years	3

4. Do you personally explain the following kinds of information to employees in your department? (Please answer all sections.)

	Yes	No
(1) Regional operating plan (in full or in part)	1	2
(2) Functional operating plan (in full or in part)	1	2
(3) Profitability and other financial information	1	2

5. In your opinion which one of the following sources provides employees with most of the information concerning the current situation within the region of relevance to their department?

Managers in their own department	1
Personnel	2
Their immediate supervisor	3
Their trade union	4
The grapevine	5
Notice boards	6
Internal publications/circulars/instructions	7

6. Within the last three years, have you participated in a management review of channels of communication within your department?

   Yes   No   Not sure
   1   2   3

7. Have your responsibilities for the communication of informa-tion to employees been explained to you (i.e. what information should be given and who should receive it)?

   Yes No
   1   2

8. Have your responsibilities for communicating information from employees to other members of management been explained to you?

   Yes No
   1   2

Part two
The audits

Audit 1

Communication and consultation

Introduction

Effective channels of communication are an essential component of good employee relations. The onus for good communications lies with management and improvements in this area can help develop a more motivated and committed workplace. What is more, the willingness of management to consult employees by means of an audit has in the past had beneficial effects in itself.

When initiating a communication and consultation audit it is desirable that the views of all sections of the workforce are taken into consideration. Hence, this section includes a set of questions for managers and supervisors as well as a set for employees.

Past audits have been successful in pinpointing those parts of an organization where communications are inadequate as well as identifying the level(s) of management at which the source of the problems arise. If you implement an audit you will be in a position to evaluate the effectiveness of your current communication and consultation arrangements and have the detailed information required to tackle the deficiencies revealed.

Audit objectives

These could be as follows:

- to evaluate the effectiveness of communications between different levels of managers and supervisors;
- to evaluate the effectiveness of communications between management and employees;
- to identify the strengths and weaknesses of current channels of communication;
- to identify areas where improvements can be made in current channels of communication;
- to evaluate the effectiveness of the joint consultative machinery; and

- to identify training needs in communication and consultation skills.

Selection of participants

If you want to obtain an accurate assessment of communications within your organization then you must seek the views of managers, supervisors, and employees. If any of these groups are omitted then only a partial picture of the situation will be obtained and the group(s) excluded are likely to take a cynical view of the findings. An audit that includes everyone will not only provide comprehensive information but will also demonstrate the organization's interest in obtaining each individual's contribution. In a communications audit it is particularly important that the results be fed back to the participants and that recommended improvements are carried out. Otherwise the whole exercise could prove to be counter-productive.

Selection and modification of questions

Before attempting to write a questionnaire from the model questions, it is strongly recommended that you read very carefully the general guidelines outlined on pages 10–13 in Part one.

There are a number of model questions for managers which are common to questions for employees. These are as follows:

MQ1 – EQ1	MQ29 – EQ18
MQ3 – EQ3	MQ30 – EQ16
MQ6 – EQ5	MQ32 – EQ20
MQ10 – EQ8	MQ33 – EQ24
MQ15 – EQ10	MQ38 – EQ29
MQ26 – EQ14	MQ40 – EQ31
MQ27 – EQ15	MQ42 – EQ32
MQ28 – EQ19	MQ43 – EQ33

It is particularly useful to be able to compare the observations of managers and employees and you are advised to retain many of the above matched questions.

The management and employee questions in this section have been selected for their general applicability. If your internal communications include such things as a formal briefing system, newsletters, a company magazine, video films, etc. then you should develop additional questions relevant to these particular channels of communication.

In past audits questions identifying department (MQ1 and EQ1) and grade (MQ2 and EQ2) have proved most useful in analysing responses. If your organization has several sites then a version of MQ3 and EQ3 should be included to enable you to evaluate communications on each site.

The questions on joint consultation have clearly been developed for unionized organizations. If you have an alternative form of formal consultative arrangement you will find that many of the model questions can be readily modified to suit your internal arrangements.

If you have more than one joint consultative committee then you should specify the particular committee you are seeking information on in the relevant questions for managers and employees.

Questions MQ6 and EQ5 ask the frequency with which managers discuss specific kinds of information with employees. You should identify the kinds of information your managers are expected to communicate and modify these questions accordingly.

Questions MQ26 – MQ32 and EQ14 – EQ22 are designed to establish the degree to which dialogue take place between managers and employees when changes in work arrangements are being introduced.

Question MQ18 is intended to see whether managers are conversant with an aspect of the legal provisions relating to the disclosure of information to trade unions. You might retain this question to see if your senior managers are aware of these provisions.

The use of 'workmates' in employee questions can be substituted by 'colleagues' if this is more appropriate for your organization.

Analysing the information collected

General guidelines summarizing the information from completed questionnaires and analysing the findings are included in Stage 6 and Stage 7 of Part one (see pages 15–21).

You should begin your analysis by using the background information of respondents, i.e. site, department, grade, to compare the answers of different groups. For each site you could compare the answers of the various departments as well as the answers of senior managers, middle managers, supervisors, white-collar staff, and manual employees. Things to look for in your analysis are:

- What information is currently being communicated and by whom?
- How well informed are your managers and supervisors?
- How well informed are your employees?
- Do some sites/departments communicate better than others?
- At what levels do communications break down?
- Are decisions discussed with employees before they are implemented?
- How effective is the joint consultative machinery?
- Are managers and employees conversant with the operation of joint consultative machinery?

Employee relations audits

Once you have analysed your audit findings you will have a snapshot of how well your communication and consultation system is operating. It is to be expected that some parts of your organization will fare better than others. You should be in a position to pinpoint the sites and departments which do least well in the audit and you should be able to identify the levels of management at which communications are breaking down. Thus you should be able to recommend action to correct identified deficiencies and direct it at specific target groups.

Communication and consultation questions for managers

MQ1* In which department do you work?

Production	1
Maintenance	2
Finance	3
Research and development	4

MQ2* What is your grade?

Grade 1 or 2	1
Grade 3-5	2
Grade 6 or above	3

MQ3 Where is your job located?

Site A	1
Site B	2
Site C	3
Site D	4

MQ4 What is the total number of employees reporting to you directly or indirectly via subordinate managers or supervisors?

5 or less	1
Between 6 and 25	2
26 or more	3

MQ5 What is your age group?

30 and under	1
31-50	2
51 and over	3

MQ6* How often do you discuss the following kinds of information with employees in your department? (Please answer all sections.)

	Frequently	Occasionally	Seldom/never
(1) Profitability and other financial information	1	2	3
(2) Budgetary and cost information	1	2	3
(3) Current and projected output/performance	1	2	3
(4) Order situation	1	2	3

(question continued)

29

	Frequently	Occasionally	Seldom/ never
(5) Quality achievement	1	2	3
(6) Changes in terms and conditions of employees, i.e. changes in provisions covering pay, holidays, overtime, etc.	1	2	3
(7) Information from joint consultative committees	1	2	3
(8) Information from health and safety committees	1	2	3

MQ7* Have your responsibilities for the communication of information to employees been fully explained to you, i.e. what information should be given and who should receive it?

Yes No Not sure
1   2   3

MQ8 In the last twelve months how many management meetings have you attended where you have been updated on recent developments within the organization?

None	1
1 or 2 meetings	2
3 or more meetings	3

MQ9 In the last twelve months, how many meetings have you held with employees in your area of responsibility to inform them of current developments within the organization?

None	1
1 or 2 meetings	2
3 or more meetings	3

MQ10* In your opinion, how do employees in your department receive *most* information concerning what is currently happening within the organization?

From managers in their department	1
From their supervisor/foreman	2
From their trade union	3
From the grapevine	4
From notice boards	5
From internal circulars/memos	6

MQ11* How would you rate the channels of information between the various levels of management in your department?

Good	1
Fairly good	2
Reasonable	3
Tend to be poor	4
Poor	5

MQ12* How would you rate the management channels of information between different departments within the organization?

Good	1
Fairly good	2
Reasonable	3
Tend to be poor	4
Poor	5

MQ13 In the last two years, have you attended a management meeting where current provisions for communicating information to employees in your department have been reviewed?

Yes	*No*	*Not sure*
1	2	3

MQ14* Are you satisfied with the following aspects of internal communications within your department?

		Yes	*No*	*Not sure*
(1)	The amount of information circulated concerning the wider organization	1	2	3
(2)	The amount of relevant information passed on to you by your boss	1	2	3
(3)	The willingness of other managers and supervisors to pass on information	1	2	3
(4)	The effectiveness of management information channels compared to those of employees (trade unions)	1	2	3

MQ15* In the last twelve months, how many times have you encountered problems in your job because relevant information was not passed on to you in good time?

(question continued)

Never   1
Once or twice   2
Three or more times   3

MQ16   In your job, do you have access to information which you consider to be confidential to members of management?

Yes   No   Not sure
1   2   3

MQ17   In the last twelve months, have you turned down a request from a trade union representative, or other employee, for information concerning the operation of your department because you considered the information to be confidential to management?

Yes   No   Not sure
1   2   3

MQ18   According to law, can trade unions be denied certain information on the grounds that this might strengthen their negotiating position with management?

Yes   No   Not sure
1   2   3

MQ19   With regard to negotiations with trade unions, is it part of your job to explain to employees the position adopted by management?

Yes   No   Not sure
1   2   3

MQ20   When negotiations relevant to employees in your department are taking place, how much information do you receive from management sources on the progress of these negotiations?

I am fully informed of the progress of
negotiations   1
I receive quite a lot of information   2
I receive a certain amount of information   3
I receive little/no information on the progress
of negotiations   4

MQ21   Is it part of your job to inform employees of changes in their terms and conditions, i.e. changes in pay, holiday entitlement, overtime provisions, etc?

Yes	No	Not sure
1	2	3

MQ22* How often do you find that (1) trade union represent-atives and (2) other employees in your department, have details of changes in terms and conditions of employ-ment before you do? (Answer both questions.)

	Always	Frequently	Occasionally	Never
(1) TU reps	1	2	3	4
(2) Other employees	1	2	3	4

MQ23 Do trade union representatives, or other employees, raise questions with you concerning the interpretation of agreements and other provisions covering terms and conditions of employment?

Yes	No
1	2

MQ24 In the last twelve months, have you experienced problems in obtaining relevant information on terms and conditions of employment in order to answer queries of employees?

Yes	No
1	2

MQ25 Do you have ready access within your department to information on terms and conditions relevant to (1) weekly paid and (2) monthly paid employees? (N.B. If you are not responsible for either of these grades ring N/A.) (Please answer both sections.)

	Yes	No	N/A
(1) weekly paid	1	2	3
(2) monthly paid	1	2	3

MQ26* In the last two years, have any major changes in work arrangements been introduced in your department, e.g. new equipment, new methods of working, reduced manning levels, management reorganization?

Yes	No
1	2

MQT27 The last time major changes in work arrangements were proposed by management in your department, what was

(question continued)

33

the general reaction of (1) trade union representatives
and (2) other employees? (Please answer both sections.)

	Co-operated	Co-operated reluctantly	Resisted pro-posals	Rejected pro-posals	Can't say
(1) TU reps	1	2	3	4	5
(2) Other employees	1	2	3	4	5

MQ28* Without new equipment, would it be possible to
introduce changes in work arrangements in your department so as to increase significantly output/performance?

Yes	*No*	*Not sure*
1	2	3

MQ29 Are there any on-going problems in your department
which you feel could be successfully tackled by a
management–employee team?

Yes	*No*	*Not sure*
1	2	3

MQ30* With regard to the last time major changes in work
arrangements were introduced in your department, which
of the following best describes the decision-making
process followed? (Ring one answer only.)

Management alone took the decisions and informed employees	1
Management took the decisions and then sought out employee views	2
Full discussions took place prior to management taking decisions	3
Joint decisions were taken by employees and management	4
Can't say	5

MQ31* In your department, how far is management prepared to
consult supervisors and to give due weight to their views
when important decisions are taken?

Management actively seeks out the views of supervisors and is willing to modify decisions in the light of these	1
Supervisors are consulted before decisions are finalized but their views are given little weight	2
Supervisors are only consulted by senior management once decisions have been finalized	3
Senior management excludes supervisors from the consultation process	4

MQ32* How far is management in your department prepared to listen to the ideas put forward by employees and to act upon them?

Management encourages employees to put
forward ideas and is willing to act upon those
which appear useful   1
Management is prepared to listen to ideas put
forward by employees but is reluctant to act
upon them   2
Employees find it difficult to get management
to listen to their ideas   3
Employees are not encouraged to put forward
ideas for consideration   4

MQ33* How often do you read the minutes of (1) the local consultative committee and (2) the regional consultative committee? (Please answer both sections.)

(1) Local consultative committee

Always	*Frequently*	*Occasionally*	*Seldom/ never*	*Minutes not available*
1	2	3	4	5

(2) Regional consultative committee

Always	*Frequently*	*Occasionally*	*Seldom/ never*	*Minutes not available*
1	2	3	4	5

MQ34* In the last twelve months, have you met with other members of management in your department to discuss the implications of any decisions taken by the joint consultative committee?

Yes   No
1   2

MQ35 In the last twelve months, has a management representative of the joint consultative committee sought your views on any subject discussed by this committee?

Yes   No
1   2

MQ36 In the last five years, have you attended a meeting of the joint consultative committee as a management representative?

(question continued)

Yes No
1 2

MQ37* Which of the following statements best describes the role of joint consultation within the organization?

Management takes the decision and uses
the consultative machinery to inform employee
representatives prior to implementation 1
Management takes decisions initially and uses
the consultative machinery to sound out
employee views before finalizing the decisions 2
Management puts forward proposals for
discussion and only takes decisions after
joint consultation has taken place 3
Decisions are made jointly by management
and employee representatives 4
Not in a position to comment 5

MQ38* Has the joint consultative machinery been explained to you, i.e. what issues are dealt with, how issues are processed, how decisions are taken?

Yes No Not sure
1 2 3

MQ39 Are you satisfied with the following aspects of joint consultation within the organization? (Please answer all sections.)

	Yes	No	Can't comment
(1) The amount of consultation that takes place between management reps on the committee and other managers/supervisors	1	2	3
(2) The amount of consultation that takes place between employees and their representatives on the committee	1	2	3
(3) The amount of information circulated from consultative meetings	1	2	3

MQ40 Do you consider that employee representatives on the joint consultative committee exert too much/too little influence on management decisions?

Exert too much influence 1
Exert too little influence 2
Influence is about right 3
Not in a position to comment 4

MQ41* With respect to important issues, how does joint consultation usually affect the final decision taken by management?

Joint consultation usually improves
the final decision   1
Joint consultation usually has an
adverse effect on the final decision   2
Joint consultation makes little/no
difference to management decisions   3
Not in a position to comment   4

MQ42* Which of the following statements best describes the effectiveness of the consultative machinery in keeping employees informed of current developments within the organization?

Employees are kept fully in the picture
by the consultative committee   1
Employees hear most of what is happening
through the consultative machinery   2
Employees have an appreciation of what is
happening through the consultative machinery   3
Employees hear very little of what is
happening through the consultative machinery   4
Employees are generally in the dark about what
is happening despite the consultative machinery   5

MQ43* Please write here any further comments you wish to make concerning internal communications and consultation.

Allow half a page for your answer.

Communication and consultation questions for employees

EQ1* In which department do you work?

Production   1
Maintenance   2
Finance   3
Research and development   4

EQ2* Is your job graded as:

Unskilled or semi-skilled   1
Skilled   2

(question continued)

37

Clerical/administrative	3
Technical	4

EQ3   Where is your job located?

Site A	1
Site B	2
Site C	3
Site D	4

EQ4   Do you normally work shifts?

Yes No

1   2

EQ5*   Does your manager/supervisor normally discuss with you the following kinds of information? (Please answer all sections.)

		Yes	*No*	*Not sure*
(1)	Profitability and other financial information	1	2	3
(2)	Budgetary and cost information	1	2	3
(3)	Current and projected output/ performance	1	2	3
(4)	Order situation	1	2	3
(5)	Quality achievement	1	2	3
(6)	Changes in terms and conditions of employment, i.e. changes in pay, holidays, allowances, etc.	1	2	3
(7)	Information from joint consultative committees	1	2	3
(8)	Information from health and safety committees	1	2	3

EQ6*   In the last twelve months, how many meetings have you attended where your manager/supervisor has updated you on recent developments within the organization?

Not attended any meetings	1
1 or 2 meetings	2
3 or more meetings	3

EQ7*   Does management in your department normally discuss its plans for the future with you and your workmates?

Yes   No

1   2

EQ8* How do you receive *most* information concerning what is happening in the organization? (Ring one answer only.)

From managers in your department   1
From your supervisor   2
From your trade union   3
From the grapevine   4
From notice boards   5
From internal publications/circulars/memos 6

EQ9 In the last twelve months have you approached a manager or supervisor with a request for information concerning the operation of your department which was turned down?

Yes   No
1   2

EQ10 In the last twelve months, how many times have you encountered problems in your job because relevant information was not passed on to you in good time?

Never   1
Once or twice   2
Three or more times   3

EQ11 When management-trade union negotiations are taking place, where do you normally get *most information* on the progress of these negotiations? (Ring one answer only.)

From management sources   1
From union sources   2
From workmates/grapevine   3
Not receive information on
negotiations   4

EQ12 If you were to receive conflicting information from management and trade union sources, which would you tend to accept as being most accurate?

Would you tend to accept the information
provided by management?   1
Would you tend to accept the information
provided by the union?   2
Not sure   3

EQ13 In the last twelve months, have you experienced any problems in obtaining information from management on

(question continued)

aspects of your terms and conditions of employment?

Yes   No
1   2

EQ14*   In the last two years, have any major changes in work arrangements been introduced in your department, e.g. new equipment, new methods of working, revised manning levels?

Yes   No
1   2

EQ15   The last time major changes in work arrangements were proposed by management in your department, what was the general reaction of (1) trade union representatives and (2) your workmates? (Please answer both sections.)

	Co-operated	Co-operated reluctantly	Resisted pro-posals	Rejected pro-posals	Can't say
(1) TU reps	1	2	3	4	5
(2) Workmates	1	2	3	4	5

EQ16*   With regard to the last time major changes in work arrangements were introduced in your department, which of the following best describes the decision-making process followed by management? (Ring one answer only.)

Management alone took the decisions and then informed employees	1
Management took the decisions and then sought out employee views	2
Full discussions took place prior to management taking decisions	3
Joint decisions were taken by employees and management	4
Can't say	5

EQ17   In the past two years, have management and employees in your department been brought together to jointly solve a particular work problem?

Yes   No   Not sure
1   2   3

EQ18   Are there any on-going problems in your department which you feel could be successfully tackled by a management–employee team?

Yes	*No*	*Not sure*
1	2	3

EQ19* Without new equipment, would it be possible to introduce changes in work arrangements in your department so as to increase significantly output/performance?

Yes	*No*	*Not sure*
1	2	3

EQ20* How far is management in your department prepared to listen to the ideas put forward by employees and to act upon them? (Ring one answer only.)

Management encourages employees to put forward ideas and is willing to act upon those which appear useful	1
Management is prepared to listen to ideas put forward by employees but is reluctant to act upon them	2
Employees find it difficult to get management to listen to their ideas	3
Employees are not encouraged to put forward ideas for consideration	4

EQ21* How would you evaluate the general attitude of management in your department with respect to involving employees in decisions of importance to their jobs? (Ring one answer only.)

Management actively seeks to involve employees in a wide range of decisions	1
Management is prepared to involve employees in decisions of direct relevance to their jobs	2
Management only seeks to involve employees in decisions when their co-operation is essential in successful implementation	3
Management is not interested in involving employees in decision-making	4

EQ22 To what extent do you agree with the following statement?
'Employees are kept well informed by management of decisions which affect their jobs.'

Agree	*Tend to agree*	*Not agree nor disagree*	*Tend to disagree*	*Disagree*
1	2	3	4	5

41

EQ23* If management in your department was to organize regular meetings which you and your workmates/ colleagues could attend, to what extent do you feel these could improve current management–employee communications?

Current management–employee communications are satisfactory and a regular meeting is not required   1
Current communications are OK but could be usefully supplemented by a regular meeting   2
Current communications are not very good and a regular meeting could significantly improve the situation   3
Current communications are poor and a regular meeting is essential   4
Can't say   5

EQ24* In your department, are the minutes of (1) the local consultative committee and (2) the regional consultative committee readily available to you? (Please answer both sections.)

(1) Local consultative committee
    Minutes are readily available   1
    Minutes are not readily available   2
    Not sure   3

(2) Regional consultative committee
    Minutes are readily available   1
    Minutes are not readily available   2
    Not sure   3

EQ25* Which *one* of the following sources normally provides you with most information regarding matters discussed at joint consultative meetings? (Ring one answer only.)

Minutes of the meetings   1
Your supervisor or manager   2
Your trade union   3
Workmates   4
Not find out information on joint consultative matters   5

EQ26* In the last twelve months, has a manager/supervisor asked your opinion concerning a matter to be discussed by the joint consultative committee?

Yes   No   Not sure
1   2   3

EQ27   In the last twelve months, has a union representative asked your opinion concerning a matter to be discussed by the joint consultative committee?

Yes   No   Not sure
1   2   3

EQ28*   In the last twelve months, has your manager/supervisor called a meeting to discuss with you and your workmates the implications of any decisions taken by the joint consultative committee?

Yes   No
1   2

EQ29*   Has the role of the joint consultative committee been explained to you, i.e. what issues are dealt with; how issues are processed; how decisions are taken?

Yes   No   Not sure
1   2   3

EQ30*   Are you satisfied with the following aspects of joint consultation within the organization? (Please answer all sections.)

	Yes	*No*	*Can't comment*
(1) Management's willingness to listen and act upon the views of employee reps	1	2	3
(2) The amount of consultation that takes place between your workmates and their reps	1	2	3
(3) The circulation of information on matters discussed at joint consultative meetings	1	2	3

EQ31   Do you consider that employee representatives on the joint consultative committee exert too much/too little influence on management decisions? (Ring one answer only.)

Exert too much influence   1
Exert too little influence   2
Influence is about right   3
Not in a position to comment   4

EQ32*   Which of the following best describes the effectiveness of the joint consultative committee in keeping your

(question continued)

workmates informed of current developments within the organization? (Ring one answer only.)

Employees are kept fully in the picture by the consultative committee	1
Employees hear most of what is happening through the consultative committee	2
Employees have an appreciation of what is happening through the consultative committee	3
Employees hear very little of what is happening through the consultative committee	4
Employees are generally in the dark about what is happening despite the consultative committee	5

EQ33*   Please write here any further comments you wish to make concerning internal communications and consultation.

Allow half a page for your answer.

Health and safety at work

Introduction

The Health and Safety at Work Act states 'it shall be the duty of every employer to ensure, so far as is reasonably practicable, the health and safety and welfare at work of all his employees'. This legislation requires all organizations with five or more employees to develop a written health and safety policy. It also includes provisions for the appointment of safety representatives, the setting up of health and safety committees, and the inspection of workplaces.

Managers and supervisors are expected to carry out the duties of the employer and it is therefore important that they fully understand their health and safety policy and arrangements for implementing it. The legislation also requires employees to take reasonable care for the health and safety of themselves and of others who could be affected by their actions. Employees also have a duty to assist the employer to fulfil his legal obligations with respect to health and safety at work. Hence, this is an area of employee relations of relevance to all who work in an organization and included in this section is one set of questions for managers and supervisors and a second set for employees.

This audit focuses on the behavioural aspects of health and safety and does not directly examine issues of a more technical nature such as those associated with a particular technology or work process. It will therefore, as it is written, provide you with a general insight into how well managers and supervisors understand their responsibilities with respect to your health and safety policy and the law. It will also reveal current practices for dealing with issues and problems that arise both from a management and employee perspective. You will be able to evaluate the impact of training provided in the past and identify outstanding training needs. However, if you are concerned to assess the effectiveness of regulations specific to your organization, questions aimed at exploring these issues should be incorporated into the audit following the pattern established in the manual.

Audit objectives

These could include a selection of the following:

- to evaluate the effectiveness of the Health and Safety Policy;
- to evaluate current standards of health and safety and to identify areas where improvements can be made;
- to assess the level of understanding of managers and employees of their responsibilities in health and safety matters;
- to determine the extent to which safety regulations are followed and safe working practices adopted;
- to assess the overall degree to which managers and employees are motivated to behave in a healthy and safe manner;
- to evaluate the impact of health and safety training; and
- to identify training needs in health and safety matters.

Selection of participants

The decision as to who will be asked to complete a questionnaire will be related to your audit objectives. On the one hand, employees at all levels within your organization have a responsibility for health and safety and your audit could therefore embrace everyone. On the other hand, some individuals by the nature of their work will have a much greater involvement in health and safety matters and your audit could effectively focus on this sub-group. Hence, you can choose a broad- or narrow-based audit. However, when selecting your participants do not automatically assume managers in office areas do not get involved in health and safety. Past audits have revealed a number of these managers who regularly deal with issues.

Selection and modification of questions

Before attempting to write a questionnaire from the model questions, it is strongly recommended that you read very carefully the general guidelines outlined on pages 10–13 in Part one.

The management and employee questions included in this section have been selected for their general applicability. However, you should incorporate some specific questions relating to your own health and safety arrangements into your questionnaires. Clearly questionnaires developed for organizations in the service sector will differ from those developed for those in metal manufacturing, heavy engineering, construction, shipbuilding, chemicals, etc. For these latter industries the model questions will have to be supplemented with some specific questions on the particular hazards encountered in the work environment.

A number of the model questions for managers are very similar to questions for employees. If you retain these questions you will be able to directly compare the answers of these two groups. These questions are as follows:

MQ1 – EQ1	MQ30 – EQ16
MQ3 – EQ3	MQ36 – EQ19
MQ12 – EQ8	MQ37 – EQ28
MQ13 – EQ28	MQ49 – EQ21
MQ28 – EQ22	MQ53 – EQ30
MQ29 – EQ24	MQ57 – EQ31

The term 'employee safety representative' is used in both management and employee questions. If you have an alternative title substitute this in the relevant questions.

There are a number of management and employee questions which refer to 'the health and safety committee'. If you have more than one committee and want information on each, then you will have to ask separate questions for each committee.

To date, questions identifying the department (MQ1 and EQ1) and the grade (MQ2 and EQ2) of respondents have proved particularly useful in analysing information from health and safety audits. You are recommended to use suitably modified versions of these questions. If you are interested in comparing the results from different sites then MQ3 and EQ3 could be used. If you have a management health and safety training course and would like to compare the answers of those who have attended with those who have not, then you might include MQ4. Past studies have indicated that working shifts can increase the incidence of accidents. If shiftwork takes place in your organization you might like to include EQ4 in your questionnaire.

If accidents are rare in your organization you may prefer to use 'In the last two years' in place of 'Within the last twelve months' in MQ6 and MQ7.

Questions MQ39 – MQ52 are only answered by respondents who have recently dealt with a health and safety issue. If you develop new questions you will have to decide whether all managers should answer them or only those who have recently handled issues and slot them into your questionnaire at the appropriate point.

If your organization has not provided any relevant training for managers in the past, do not automatically exclude MQ55. It could prove useful if respondents confirm this situation in your audit especially if you have to make out a case for training resources at a later date.

Questions EQ22 and EQ24 refer to 'workmates', you might choose 'colleagues' as an alternative wording.

Analysing the information collected

General guidelines on summarizing the information from completed questionnaires and analysing the findings have been explained in Stages 6 and 7 of Part one (see pages 15–21).

You should begin your initial analysis by using the background information of respondents, e.g. site, department, and grade to compare the answers of different groups. For each site you could compare the answers of different departments and those of senior managers, middle managers, supervisors, white-collar staff, and manual employees. Questions you should bear in mind during your analysis are:

- What problems arise and how frequently are they encountered?
- Which groups are most at risk?
- To what extent are accident reporting procedures understood and followed?
- How effective is the health and safety policy?
- How well do managers and employees understand their responsibilities?
- How effective are safety representatives and the health and safety committee?
- How well is health and safety information communicated?
- Who has received training and what impact has it had?
- Is there scope for improvements in health and safety provisions and, if so, where?

Once initial analysis has been carried out and significant findings noted, secondary analysis can be done. For example, if you find that twenty-three supervisors have reported particular difficulty in handling issues, you can then determine whether members of this group have particularly active safety representatives, whether they have been in contact with their safety officer and whether they have received training.

If it appears from the audit that some departments or work groups are more prone than others to encounter health and safety problems, it may be advantageous to involve those groups at most risk in the analysis of the findings. The development of action plans by such work groups to deal with the problems identified could be an effective way of bringing about the desired improvements.

Health and safety questions for managers

MQ1* In which department do you work?

Production	1
Maintenance	2
Finance	3
Research and development	4

MQ2* What is your management grade?

Grade 1 or 2	1
Grade 3–5	2
Grade 6 or above	3

MQ3 Where is your job located?

Site A	1
Site B	2
Site C	3
Site D	4

MQ4 When did you attend the internal course entitled 'Health and Safety for Managers'?

Not attended course	1
Within the last 2 years	2
Within the last 2–5 years	3
More than 5 years ago	4
Not sure	5

MQ5 What is the total number of employees reporting to you directly or indirectly via subordinate managers or supervisors?

5 or less employees	1
6–15 employees	2
16–25 employees	3
More than 25 employees	4

MQ6 Within the last twelve months, how many employees in your area of responsibility have had an accident at work which required first aid or other medical treatment?

Three or more employees	*One or two employees*	*None*
1	2	3

MQ7   Within the last twelve months, how many employees in your area of responsibility had an accident at work which caused them to have one or more days off work?

Three or more employees	*One or two employees*	*None*
1	2	3

MQ8   Is there an accident report book in your department?

Yes	*No*	*Not sure*
1	2	3

MQ9   Should an accident report form be completed for the following situations? (Please answer all sections.)

	Yes	*No*	*Not sure*
(1) Accidents involving serious injury causing time off work	1	2	3
(2) Accidents involving minor injury requiring first aid but no time off work	1	2	3
(3) Accidents not involving injury but causing damage to property or equipment	1	2	3

MQ10   Is it necessary to complete an accident report form for an accident on company premises if the only person involved was a member of the general public and he/she was solely to blame?

Yes	*No*	*Not sure*
1	2	3

MQ11   Is it necessary to complete an accident report form for an accident on company premises if the only person involved was a contractor and he/she was solely to blame?

Yes	*No*	*Not sure*
1	2	3

MQ12*   In the last twelve months, how many times have you encountered the following situations within the organization? (Please answer all sections.)

	Never	*Once or twice*	*Three or more times*
(1) Machinery being operated with safety guards removed	1	2	3

(2)	Plant/equipment that is hazardous to use	1	2	3
(3)	Smoking in non-smoking areas	1	2	3
(4)	Breaking of the regulations covering the wearing of hard hats	1	2	3
(5)	Breaking the regulations covering the wearing of goggles	1	2	3
(6)	Breaking the regulations covering the wearing of safety shoes	1	2	3
(7)	Cranes and hoists being operated in an unsafe manner	1	2	3
(8)	Unsafe work platforms/ladders	1	2	3
(9)	Hazards arising because of horse-play by employees	1	2	3
(10)	Hazards arising from the unsafe working practices of subcontractors	1	2	3

MQ13* How did the majority of employees in your area of responsibility react the *last* time an emergency fire alarm was set off in your department?

Stopped work and went to see what was happening	1
Stopped work and waited for instructions	2
Stopped work and evacuated the building	3
Carried on working	4
Not sure	5

MQ14 In your area of responsibility, do you personally explain to new employees the health and safety hazards that they could encounter in their jobs and the safe working practices to be followed?

Yes   No
1   2

MQ15 In your area of responsibility, has there been a systematic identification of the health and safety hazards encountered by employees?

Yes   No   Not sure
1   2   3

MQ16* Do new employees in your department always receive training in the health and safety aspects of their job within their first week of employment?

Yes   No   Not sure
1   2   3

MQ17* Does health and safety training for new employees in your department always include the following? (Please answer all sections.)

		Yes	No	Not sure
(1)	Management and employee responsibilities for health and safety	1	2	3
(2)	Role of safety representative/health and safety committee	1	2	3
(3)	Safety rules and procedures	1	2	3
(4)	Use of protective clothing	1	2	3
(5)	Emergency procedures in the event of fire	1	2	3
(6)	Hazards encountered in jobs	1	2	3

MQ18 When new machinery/equipment is introduced in your department, what priority is given to the health and safety aspects of operating it?

Health and safety aspects are given the highest priority	1
Health and safety aspects are considered of equal importance to those of production	2
Health and safety aspects are of secondary importance to getting the machinery/equipment in use	3
Health and safety aspects are often overlooked	4
Not in a position to comment	5

MQ19* Do you possess, or have ready access to, a copy of the health and safety policy relevant to your department?

Possess a copy	1
Heavy ready access to a copy	2
No ready access to a copy	3
Not sure	4

MQ20* Have the provisions of the health and safety policy been explained to you, i.e. roles of management, employee representatives, and health and safety committees?

Yes	No	Not sure
1	2	3

MQ21 With regard to the content of the health and safety policy, which of the following best describes your level of understanding?

Fully understand all aspects of the policy	1
Understand most aspects	2

Have some understanding   3
Have little/no knowledge of the policy   4
Not sure   5

MQ22*   With respect to health and safety matters, have you been
        informed of your responsibilities and the responsibilities
        of other managers including personnel and safety
        specialists?
        Have been informed of responsibilities and
        am conversant with them   1
        Have been informed but cannot remember
        them very well   2
        Have been informed but have forgotten them   3
        Have not been informed of responsibilities   4
        Not sure if the information has been
        given to me   5

MQ23   In your department, is there any potentially dangerous
        machinery/equipment currently in use, which given the
        necessary financial resources, you would replace?

        Yes   No   Can't say
         1   2   3

MQ24   Are there any on-going problems in your department
        where the advice of a health and safety specialist would
        be of benefit?

        Yes   No   Not sure
         1   2   3

        If *Yes*, please give details ....
        ....
        ....

MQ25   How many management meetings have you attended in
        the last twelve months where health and safety matters
        were discussed?
        None   1
        1 or 2   2
        3 or more   3

MQ26   In the last twelve months, has your view been sought on
        any issue discussed by a health and safety committee?

        Yes   No
         1   2

MQ27 How frequently are meetings held of the health and safety committee relevant to your department?

Weekly	1
Fortnightly	2
Monthly	3
Quarterly	4
Once or twice a year	5
Stopped holding meetings	6
Not sure	7

MQ28* How often do you read the minutes of the health and safety committee relevant to your department?

Always	1
Frequently	2
50% of the time	3
Occasionally	4
Never	5
Minutes not available	6

MQ29 In your opinion, how effective is the health and safety committee in the prevention of accidents?

Very effective	1
Quite effective	2
Not very effective	3
Has minimal impact	4
Can't say	5

MQ30* Do you know who is the safety representative with responsibility for your area of work?

Yes   No   Not sure
1   2   3

MQ31 Can a safety representative carrying out a workplace inspection in your area of responsibility, insist that you accompany him/her during the inspection?

Yes   No   Not sure
1   2   3

MQ32 Within the last twelve months, has a workplace safety inspection been carried out in your area of work by an employee safety representative?

Yes   No   Not sure
1   2   3

MQ33   Does the company give employee safety representatives
        paid time off work to attend a TUC approved training
        course?

        Yes   No   Not sure
        1   2   3

MQ34*   Have you been informed of (1) the responsibilities of
        safety representatives and (2) the facilities to be made
        available to these representatives? (Please answer both
        sections.)

        (1) Responsibilities of safety reps
           Have been informed and am conversant with them   1
           Have been informed but do not remember them
           very well   2
           Have been informed but have forgotten them   3
           Have not been informed   4
           Not sure if the information has been given to me   5

        (2) Facilities available to safety reps
           Have been informed and am conversant with them   1
           Have been informed but cannot remember them
           very well   2
           Have been informed but have forgotten them   3
           Have not been informed   4
           Not sure if the information has been given to me   5

MQ35   Can individual managers or supervisors be served with an
        Improvement Notice by an officer of the Health and Safe-
        ty Executive?

        Yes   No   Not sure
        1   2   3

MQ36*   How would you evaluate the respective levels of
        knowledge of supervisors and trade union representatives
        in health and safety matters?

        Supervisors are generally better informed
        than trade union representatives   1
        Trade union representatives are generally
        better informed than supervisors   2
        There is little difference in the levels
        of knowledge of supervisors and trade
        union representatives   3
        Not in a position to comment   4

MQ37*   How often do the following situations occur in your

                                        (question continued)

55

department? (Please answer all sections.)

	Often	Quite often	Occasion- ally	Never/ rarely
(1) Employees adopting a 'couldn't care less' attitude to safety	1	2	3	4
(2) Employees not recognizing potential health and safety hazards	1	2	3	4
(3) Pressure on managers and supervisors to turn a 'blind eye' to health and safety regulations	1	2	3	4
(4) Inadequate consideration given to health and safety aspects when introducing new methods of working	1	2	3	4
(5) Dangerous work practices followed by contractors	1	2	3	4
(6) Inadequate supply of safety equipment/clothing	1	2	3	4

MQ38* During the last twelve months, how often on average have you had occasion to deal with a health and safety matter?

Daily	1
Weekly	2
Monthly	3
Occasionally	4
Never	5

Procedure: If the answer to MQ38 is never, proceed to MQ53, otherwise proceed to MQ39.

MQ39 In an average week, how much time do you spend dealing with health and safety matters?

Less than 1 hour	1
From 1 hour to half a day	2
Over half a day	3

MQ40 During the last twelve months, has your personal involvement in health and safety matters grown, diminished or remained relatively constant?

Grown	1
Diminished	2
Relatively constant	3

56

MQ41* During the last twelve months, have you dealt with a safety representative regarding a health and safety issue?

Yes   No
1   2

MQ42 In the last twelve months, have you personally approached a safety representative to examine jointly an issue in your department?

Yes   No
1   2

MQ43 Which of the following statements best describes the general attitude of safety representatives in your department? (Ring one answer only.)

They show little interest in health and safety matters	1
They only show an interest when problems are brought to them	2
They keep their eyes open for potential hazards but are sensible in the issues they raise with management	3
They are very active and pursue every minor issue	4
Not in a position to comment	5

MQ44 To what extent do you agree/disagree with the following statements concerning the current attitudes of safety representatives? (Please answer all sections.)

	Agree	*Tend to agree*	*Not agree nor disagree*	*Tend to disagree*	*Dis-agree*
(1) Reps seek solutions to problems from a trade union view-point rather than seeking what is best from a health and safety perspective	1	2	3	4	5
(2) Reps readily accept joint responsibility with management for improving current health and safety standards	1	2	3	4	5
(3) Reps see their main role as processing health and safety					

(question continued)

	Agree	Tend to agree	Not agree nor disagree	Tend to disagree	Dis-agree
grievances raised by employees	1	2	3	4	5
(4) Reps seek to resolve health and safety issues with management by negotiation rather than consultation	1	2	3	4	5

MQ45 Does the law require that in fully unionized establishments all safety representatives must also be shop stewards?

Yes   No   Not sure
1   2   3

MQ46 If a safety representative fails to act upon a report from an employee concerning a dangerous working practice and an accident occurs, does the representative have immunity against legal proceedings?

Yes   No   Not sure
1   2   3

MQ47* In the last twelve months, how many times have you stopped employees working for health and safety reasons?

Never   1
Once or twice   2
3 or more times   3

MQ48 In the last twelve months, have you instructed employees not to operate any specific plant or equipment which you considered to be hazardous?

Yes   No
1   2

MQ49 During the last twelve months, have employees in your area of responsibility refused to carry out any of their normal duties because of a health and safety hazard?

Yes   No
1   2

MQ50 In the last twelve months, have you (1) informally reprimanded or (2) taken disciplinary action against an employee for breaking health and safety rules? (Please answer both sections.)

58

		Yes	*No*
(1)	Informally reprimanded	1	2
(2)	Disciplinary action	1	2

MQ51 During the last twelve months, have you contacted any internal safety specialists, e.g. safety officer, for advice or assistance in the handling of a health and safety matter?

Yes *No*

1 2

MQ52 How would you evaluate the following internal provisions related to health and safety? (Please answer all sections.)

		Good	Fairly good	Not very good	Inade-quate	Can't say
(1)	The content of health and safety policies and procedures	1	2	3	4	5
(2)	The training of managers/supervisors in health and safety matters	1	2	3	4	5
(3)	Management sources of information on accident prevention, health and safety committee decisions, new legislation, etc.	1	2	3	4	5
(4)	The advisory service provided by the health and safety officer	1	2	3	4	5

MQ53* To what extent do you feel that there is scope for improving the health and safety standards in your department? (Please ring one answer only.)

A lot of improvement is possible	1
Significant improvement is possible	2
A reasonable amount of improvement is possible	3
Only limited improvement is possible	4
There is little or no scope for improvement	5
Not in a position to comment	6

MQ54 When did the organization last provide you with off-the-job training (management seminars, briefings, courses, etc.) in internal health and safety policies, procedures, and associated legislation?

(question continued)

Within the last 2 years	1
From 2 to 5 years ago	2
Over 5 years ago	3
No off-the-job training received	4

MQ55* Given the needs of your job, how adequate has been the training you have received in health and safety matters?

Full training received	1
Training in most aspects	2
Some rather basic training received	3
Little or no training received	4

MQ56 Given the nature of your job, what priority would you give to your training needs in health and safety policies, procedures, and associated legislation?

High priority	1
Medium priority	2
Low priority	3
No training required	4

MQ57 Please outline here any further comments you would like to make concerning health and safety within the company and training you have received to date.

Allow half a page for your answer.

Health and safety questions for employees

EQ1* In which department do you work?

Production	1
Maintenance	2
Finance	3
Research and development	4

EQ2* Is your job graded as:

Unskilled or semi-skilled?	1
Skilled?	2
Clerical/administrative?	3
Technical?	4

EQ3 Where is your job located?

Site A	1
Site B	2

Site C		3
Site D		4

EQ4   Do you normally work shifts?

Yes   *No*
1   2

EQ5   What is your age group?

25 years or under	1
26–50 years	2
Over 50 years	3

EQ6   What is your total length of service with the organization?

Less than 6 months	1
6 months to 2 years	2
3–5 years	3
More than 5 years	4

EQ7   Are you currently a safety representative?

Yes   *No*
1   2

EQ8*   In the last twelve months, how many times have you encountered the following situations within the organization? (Please answer all sections.)

		Never	*Once or twice*	*Three or more times*
(1)	Machinery being operated with safety guards removed	1	2	3
(2)	Plant or equipment that is hazardous to use	1	2	3
(3)	Smoking in non-smoking areas	1	2	3
(4)	Breaking of the regulations covering the wearing of hard hats	1	2	3
(5)	Breaking of the regulations covering the wearing of goggles	1	2	3
(6)	Breaking of the regulations covering the wearing of safety shoes	1	2	3
(7)	Cranes and hoists being operated in an unsafe manner	1	2	3
(8)	Unsafe work platforms or ladders	1	2	3
(9)	Hazards arising from horse-play by employees	1	2	3

(question continued)

61

		Never	Once or twice	Three or more times
(10)	Hazards arising from the unsafe working practices of subcontractors	1	2	3

EQ9* In the last twelve months, have you been asked to carry out a potentially dangerous task which you had never done before, without being fully briefed on the appropriate safe working method to be followed?

Yes *No*

1 2

EQ10* In the last twelve months, have you been given a potentially dangerous task which you were not confident you could carry out safely?

Yes *No*

1 2

EQ11* Which *one* of the following usually provides new employees in your department with *most* information on the key health and safety aspects of the job? (Ring one answer only.)

Safety officer	1
Training department	2
Supervisor	3
Manager	4
Safety representative	5
Workmates	6
Safety notices/posters	7
Can't say	8

EQ12* In health and safety training provided for you, were the following items covered? (Please answer all sections.)

		Yes	No	Not sure
(1)	Employee and management responsibilities	1	2	3
(2)	Role of safety representatives and the health and safety committee	1	2	3
(3)	Safety rules and procedures	1	2	3
(4)	Use of protective clothing	1	2	3
(5)	Emergency procedures in the event of fire	1	2	3
(6)	Hazards encountered in your job	1	2	3

EQ13* To what extent does management in your department provide newly recruited employees with training in the health and safety aspects of their job?

Full training is provided by the department in all aspects of health and safety	1
Training is provided in the most important aspects	2
Some training is provided but certain key aspects of health and safety are not covered	3
Little or no relevant health and safety training is provided by the department	4
Can't say	5

EQ14* Are you unsure about the safe working practice to follow with any equipment or machinery you have to use in your job?

Yes   No
1   2

If *Yes*, please give details ....
....
....

EQ15 Are you unsure about the health and safety aspects of handling any chemicals/toxic substances you come into contact with in your job?

Yes   No
1   2

If *Yes*, please give details ....
....
....

EQ16 Do you know who is the employee safety representative for your work area?

Yes   No   Not sure
1   2   3

EQ17 Has the role of the safety representative been explained to you?

Yes   No   Not sure
1   2   3

EQ18 In the last twelve months, how often have you and/or your workmates raised a health and safety issue with your safety representative?

(question continued)

Never	1
Once or twice	2
Three or more times	3

EQ19* How would you evaluate the respective levels of knowledge of supervisors and trade union representatives in health and safety matters?

Supervisors are generally better informed than trade union representatives	1
Trade union representatives are generally better informed than supervisors	2
There is little difference in the levels of knowledge of supervisors and trade union representatives	3
Not in a position to comment	4

EQ20 In the last twelve months, how often have you and/or your workmates raised a health and safety issue with a manager/supervisor?

Never	1
Once or twice	2
Three or more times	3

EQ21 During the last twelve months, have you refused to carry out any of your normal duties because of a health and safety hazard?

Yes   No

1   2

EQ22* How often do you read the minutes of the health and safety committee relevant to your department?

Always	1
Frequently	2
About half the time	3
Occasionally	4
Infrequently/never	5
Minutes not available	6

EQ23 In the last twelve months, has a manager or supervisor discussed with you and your workmates any issue that was raised at a meeting of the health and safety committee?

Yes   No   Not sure

1   2   3

EQ24* In your opinion, how effective is the health and safety committee in the prevention of accidents?

Very effective   1
Quite effective   2
Not very effective   3
Has very little impact   4
Can't say   5

EQ25 In the last twelve months, has a safety representative discussed with you and your workmates any issue raised at a meeting of the health and safety committee?

Yes   No   Not sure
  1   2   3

EQ26* How do you receive *most* information of relevance to your job on issues discussed by the health and safety committee? (Ring one answer only.)

From your manager/supervisor   1
From your safety rep/trade union   2
From minutes of meetings/memos/
circulars, etc.   3
From workmates/grapevine   4
Not receive information   5

EQ27 In the last twelve months, have you encountered any dangerous hazards in your job which were caused by the unsafe working practices of contractors?

Yes   No
  1   2

EQ28* How often do the following situations occur in your department?

	Often	*Quite often*	*Occasion-ally*	*Never/ rarely*
(1) Employee adopting a 'couldn't care less' attitude to safety rules and procedures	1	2	3	4
(2) Inconsistent application of health and safety rules by managers and supervisors	1	2	3	4
(3) Management pressure on employees to ignore health and safety rules to get the job done	1	2	3	4

(question continued)

	Often	Quite often	Occasion-ally	Never/ rarely
(4) Laid down safe working methods too impractical to apply	1	2	3	4
(5) Inadequate consideration given by management to health and safety aspects when intro-ducing new equipment/ machinery	1	2	3	4
(6) Dangerous work practices followed by contractors	1	2	3	4
(7) Inadequate supply of safety equipment/ clothing	1	2	3	4

EQ29* How did you react the *last* time an emergency fire alarm was set off in your department?

Stopped work and went to see what was happening	1
Stopped work and waited for instructions	2
Stopped work and left the building	3
Carried on working	4
Not sure	5

EQ30* To what extent do you feel that there is scope for improving the health and safety standards in your department?

A lot of improvement is possible	1
Significant improvement is possible	2
A reasonable amount of improvement is possible	3
Only limited improvement is possible	4
There is little or no scope for improvement	5
Not in a position to comment	6

EQ31* Please write here any further comments you wish to make concerning health and safety matters in your department.

Allow half a page for your answer.

Audit 3

Equality of opportunity

Introduction

It is illegal in the UK for organizations to discriminate in their employment policies and practices on the basis of race or sex. This has important implications for decisions on recruitment, promotion, training opportunities, pay, and other matters. Organizations seeking to follow the requirements of legislation expect their managers and supervisors to take decisions in these key areas of employee relations in a non-discriminatory manner. Hence, it is important that discriminatory practices are not being followed and that line managers understand their responsibilities. An equal opportunity audit is a useful means of finding out whether problems exist and if your organization has a formal equal opportunities policy then an audit will provide an indication of its effectiveness.

Most employment decisions are the responsibility of management and it is therefore important that line managers provide information for the audit. However, employees are also likely to have views on the extent to which non-discriminatory practices are followed and these could vary greatly from those of managers. Hence, model questions are provided for both managers and employees.

Audit objectives

Participants must not perceive the audit as a witchhunt designed to identify and punish those who are discriminating. Objectives should therefore be seen as constructive and could be a selection of the following:

- to determine the effectiveness of the equal opportunities policy;
- to identify areas where improvements can be made in equal opportunity provisions;
- to determine line managers' awareness of their responsibilities;
- to examine current practices in selection for recruitment and promotion;
- to identify management training needs; and

- to identify areas where improvements could be made in the employment opportunities of women and members of ethnic minority groups.

Selection of participants

The way in which management takes decisions on the selection of individuals for recruitment, promotion, and training is clearly relevant to employees who are affected by these decisions. Hence, an audit will be relevant for all sections of the workforce in your organization. If you are actively seeking to promote equality of opportunity and to raise awareness of the issues concerned, then you should consider including as wide a coverage of the workforce as is possible. However, if your objectives are more limited then you might focus your audit solely on those managers who are most involved in recruitment and promotion decisions.

Selection and modification of questions

Before attempting to write a questionnaire from the model questions, it is strongly recommended that you read very carefully the general guidelines outlined on pages 10–13 in Part one.

In this section there are a number of management and employee questions relating to racial discrimination which use the terms 'member of a black ethnic minority group' and 'black person'. If these are not acceptable within your organization select an alternative terminology.

There are a number of model questions for managers which are similar to questions for employees thus offering the opportunity of directly comparing the views of the two groups. They are as follows:

MQ2 – EQ1	MQ31 – EQ13
MQ3 – EQ3	MQ39 – EQ17
MQ7 – EQ5	MQ40 – EQ19
MQ23 – EQ6	MQ43 – EQ22
MQ24 – EQ7	MQ46 – EQ24
MQ25 – EQ8	MQ47 – EQ25
MQ26 – EQ10	MQ50 – EQ27
MQ29 – EQ11	MQ53 – EQ28

A number of questions refer to the 'equal opportunities policy (legislation)'. If you have a policy refer only to this; if you do not, refer only to the legislation.

With respect to questions seeking background information of respondents, i.e. MQ1 – MQ8, past experience indicates that suitably modified versions of MQ1 and MQ2 are usually of most assistance in the analysis of findings. If you suspect that women managers will answer differently to men, then include MQ3. If your organization has a number of sites then MQ7 should be included.

Questions MQ9, MQ11, and MQ12 ask respondents whether they 'have an involvement in' certain decisions of relevance to equal opportunities. You might prefer to change the wording to whether they 'are consulted about'.

Questions MQ17 – MQ22 inclusive are only answered by respondents who interview job applicants. Any new questions specifically designed for this sub-group of managers should be slotted in here.

In questions MQ34 and MQ41 'in the last two years' has been specified; you might prefer 'in the last twelve months'.

There are five questions designed to provide information on the background of employees, i.e. EQ1 – EQ5. The question identifying department (EQ1) has generally proved most useful in the past. If you wish to differentiate between the answers of men and women then EQ3 is relevant and if you employ significant numbers of employees who belong to a racial minority group, then a modified version of EQ4 could prove useful.

Questions EQ8, EQ9, and EQ10 seek similar information; select only one of them.

Questions EQ19, EQ20, and EQ26 refer to 'workmates'; for white-collar groups 'colleagues' might be preferable.

Analysing the information collected

General guidelines for summarizing the information from completed questionnaires and analysing the findings are included in Stages 6 and 7 of Part one (see pages 15–21).

You should use the background information questions, e.g. job, grade, department, site, sex to compare the responses of different groups. Questions you should bear in mind are:

- Do your procedures for selecting successful job applicants meet legislative requirements?
- To what extent are your employment practices perceived to be non-discriminatory?
- Are there any differences in views of managers, supervisors, and employees with respect to the existence of discriminatory practices?
- Are the employment opportunities for women equal to those of men?
- What problems are encountered in achieving equality of opportunity?

- How effective is your equal opportunities policy?
- To what extent do managers understand the provisions of your equal opportunity policy and the law?
- Can training help improve the current situation?

After carrying out your initial analysis you might like to focus on the responses of certain sub-groups. For example, a closer examination of the answers of managers who interview or shortlist external job candidates, could prove valuable. If you have provided training in the past then a comparison of the responses of those who have received training with those who have not will provide an insight into the effectiveness of your training.

Once your analysis has been completed and the key findings identified, you should be in a position to judge how far equality of opportunity exists within your organization.

Equal opportunity questions for managers

MQ1* What is the grade of your job?

Grade 1 or 2	1
Grade 3–5	2
Grade 6 or above	3

MQ2* In which department do you work?

Production	1
Engineering	2
Finance	3
Marketing	4
Research and development	5

MQ3 What is your sex?

Male	1
Female	2

MQ4 How many employees report to you directly or indirectly via subordinate managers and supervisors?

5 or less	1
Between 6 and 25	2
26 or more	3

MQ5 What are the sexes of employees in your area of responsibility?

All are male	1
All are female	2
Both male and female	3

MQ6 Do you manage or supervise any employee who is a member of an ethnic minority group?

Yes	1
No	2
Not sure	3

MQ7 Where is your job located?

Site A	1
Site B	2
Site C	3
Site D	4

MQ8 What is your age group?

30 years and under	1

31–50	2
51 years and over	3

MQ9 Do you have an involvement in decisions regarding employee specifications for jobs in your department, e.g. requirements of age, experience, education?

Yes   No
1   2

MQ10* Is it part of your job to recommend employees for (1) training or (2) promotion? (Please answer both sections.)

(1) Recommend for training

Yes   No   Not sure
1   2   3

(2) Recommend for promotion

Yes   No   Not sure
1   2   3

MQ11 Do you have an involvement in the wording of internal or external job vacancy advertisements?

Yes   No
1   2

MQ12 Do you have an involvement in decisions concerning where job vacancies will be advertised externally, e.g. newspapers, Job Centres, private employment agencies?

Yes   No
1   2

MQ13* Is your advice or assistance sought in the sorting of internal or external job applications, i.e. in choosing who is/is not to be considered for interview?

Yes   No
1   2

MQ14 Is your opinion sought on the relative merits of job candidates for your section/department?

Yes   No
1   2

MQ15 Can you refuse to accept a person recruited for your section/department if you do not consider him/her to be suitable?

Yes　*No*　*Not sure*

1　　2　　　3

MQ16* Do you interview applications (internal or external) for jobs?

Yes　*No*

1　　2

Procedure: If your answer to MQ16 is *No*, please proceed to MQ23 otherwise proceed to MQ17

MQ17* At interviews of job applicants attended by you, how often is there a personnel specialist present?

Always	1
Frequently	2
50% of the time	3
Occasionally	4
Never	5

MQ18* With respect to interviews of job applicants attended by you, are the reasons for all unsuccessful applications fully recorded?

Yes　*No*　*Not sure*

1　　2　　　3

MQ19* When interviewing job applicants, do you normally ask questions on the following? (Please answer all sections.)

	Yes	*No*
(1) Health and physical fitness	1	2
(2) Sickness absence in previous job	1	2
(3) Marital status	1	2
(4) Domestic arrangements for school holidays and sickness of children	1	2
(5) Friends or relatives currently employed by the organization	1	2

MQ20 In your opinion which *one* of the following produces the most suitable job applicants for your department/section? (Ring one answer only.)

Local Job Centre	1
Private employment agencies	2

(question continued)

Newspaper advertisements 3
Informal network of friends
and relations of current employees 4
Other please specify 5 ....
....

MQ21 Is it normal in your department to give preference to job applicants personally recommended by current employees?

Yes *No* *Not sure*
1 2 3

MQ22* Has the organization provided you with training in interviewing/selection techniques?

Yes *No* *Not sure*
1 2 3

MQ23 In your opinion are there any jobs in your department which women could not carry out?

Yes *No*
1 2

If *Yes*, please specify ....
....
....

MQ24 In your opinion are there any jobs in your department which men could not carry out?

Yes *No*
1 2

If *Yes*, please specify ....
....
....

MQ25* Do you believe that there are members of management in your organization who consciously or subconsciously discriminate against women when recruiting or promoting?

Yes *No* *Can't say*
1 2 3

MQ26* To what extent do you agree with the statement: 'Within the organization, a woman has an equal chance of achieving promotion to a senior management position as a man with similar ability'?

Agree	*Tend to agree*	*Not agree nor disagree*	*Tend to disagree*	*Disagree*
1	2	3	4	5

MQ27 Are there certain jobs in your department for which only men are traditionally recruited?

Yes	*No*
1	2

Procedure: If the answer to MQ27 is *Yes* proceed to MQ28, otherwise proceed to MQ29

MQ28 To what extent do the following hinder the *recruitment* of women into jobs in your department traditionally carried out by men? (Please answer all sections.)

	Is a definite hindrance	*Tends to be a hindrance*	*Is not a hindrance*
(1) Physical demands of work	1	2	3
(2) Working conditions	1	2	3
(3) Job specifications, i.e. past work experience, educational, and technical qualifications	1	2	3
(4) Family commitments outside work	1	2	3
(5) The filling of vacant jobs by applicants recommended by current employees	1	2	3
(6) Management's reluctance to consider women for jobs traditionally carried out by men	1	2	3
(7) The reluctance of women to apply for jobs	1	2	3

Note: If there are other important factors hindering the recruitment of women, then please give details:

....

....

MQ29 To what extent do the following hinder the *promotion* of women to management positions within the organization? (Please answer all sections.)

	Is a definite hindrance	Tends to be a hindrance	Is not a hindrance
(1) Internal training opportunities available to women	1	2	3
(2) Formal qualifications required for management jobs, e.g. degree, HND, A levels	1	2	3
(3) Family commitments outside work	1	2	3

Note: If there are other important factors hindering the promotion of women, then please give details:

....

....

....

MQ30 If a particular job involves strenuous physical work is that sufficient justification in law for restricting the job to men alone?

Yes	No	Not sure
1	2	3

MQ31 Are there any jobs in your department where (1) single, (2) married candidates are preferred? (Please answer both sections.)

	Yes	No
(1) Job(s) where single person is preferred	1	2
(2) Job(s) where married person is preferred	1	2

Note: Please give details of job(s) concerned:

....

....

MQ32* Are there any members of an ethnic minority group employed in your area of work?

Yes	No
1	2

MQ33   Are employees in your area of work required to deal with members of the public?

Yes   No
1   2

MQ34   In the last two years, have any problems arisen between customers (or members of the public) and employees in your section/department where racial prejudice was a factor?

Yes   No   Not sure
1   2   3

MQ35   Are there any jobs in your section/department where the employment of a member of a black ethnic minority group could be a source of embarrassment?

Yes   No   Not sure
1   2   3

If *Yes*, please give details of jobs ....

....

....

MQ36*   To what extent do the following hinder the *recruitment* of black persons into jobs in your section/department? (Please answer all sections.)

	Is a definite hindrance	*Tends to be a hindrance*	*Is not a hindrance*
(1) The filling of jobs by applicants recommended by current employees	1	2	3
(2) The practice for advertising job vacancies	1	2	3
(3) The reluctance of black persons to apply for jobs	1	2	3
(4) The ability of black applicants to meet job specifications, e.g. past work experience, educational, and technical qualifications	1	2	3
(5) The reluctance of members of the public/ customers to deal with black persons	1	2	3

(question continued)

	Is a definite hindrance	*Tends to be a hindrance*	*Is not a hindrance*
(6) Management's reluctance to employ black persons in sensitive areas	1	2	3

Note: If there are other important factors hindering the recruitment of black persons, then please give details

....

....

MQ37 To what extent do the following hinder the *promotion* of black persons to management positions within the organization? (Please answer all sections.)

	Is a definite hindrance	*Tend to be a hindrance*	*Is not a hindrance*
(1) Internal training opportunities available to black persons	1	2	3
(2) Formal qualifications for management positions, i.e. degree, HND, membership of a professional association	1	2	3
(3) The reluctance of black persons to apply for management jobs	1	2	3
(4) The resistance of employees to being managed/supervised by a black person	1	2	3
(5) The organization's reluctance to appoint a black person to a managerial position	1	2	3

Note: If there are other important factors which hinder the promotion of black persons then please give details

....

....

....

MQ38* Do you believe that there are members of management in your department who consciously or subconsciously discriminate against members of black minority groups when recruiting/promoting?

Yes   No   Can't say

1   2   3

MQ39*   To what extent do you agree with the statement:
'A member of a black ethnic minority group has an
equal opportunity of obtaining employment with
the organization as other applicants with similar
ability'?

Agree	Tend to agree	Neither agree nor disagree	Tend to disagree	Disagree
1	2	3	4	5

MQ40   Do you believe that a black employee would be readily
accepted by work groups under your control?

Yes   No   Not sure

1   2   3

MQ41*   Within the last two years, have you in your capacity as a
manager/supervisor had to deal with any of the following
complaints regarding alleged unfair treatment on the
grounds of race, sex, or marital status? (Please answer all
sections.)

	Yes	No	Not sure
(1) Alleged unfair treatment on the grounds of race	1	2	3
(2) Alleged unfair treatment on the grounds of sex	1	2	3
(3) Alleged unfair treatment on the grounds of marital status	1	2	3

MQ42   Is it always justifiable to reject an application for
employment on the grounds that the candidate's grasp of
the English language is not good?

Yes   No   Not sure

1   2   3

MQ43   With respect to your department, to what extent do you
agree/disagree with the following statements? (Please
answer all sections.)

(question continued)

	Agree	Tend to agree	Not agree nor disagree	Tend to disagree	Dis-agree
(1) White applicants for jobs have no advantage over black applicants with similar ability	1	2	3	4	5
(2) In recruitment, job applicants with families are favoured over applicants who do not	1	2	3	4	5
(3) As a result of the Sex Discrimination Act (or equal opportunities policy) all internal hindrances to women achieving senior management positions have been removed	1	2	3	4	5
(4) Men employed on manual work would resist efforts of management to have women work alongside them	1	2	3	4	5
(5) Work groups comprised of all-white employees would resist management efforts to introduce black workers into these groups	1	2	3	4	5

MQ44* What is the *minimum* period of continuous service that an employee must have served before he/she is entitled to process at an industrial tribunal a claim for unfair dismissal on the grounds of racial or sexual discrimination? (Ring one answer only.)

13 weeks	1
26 weeks	2
1 year	3
2 years	4
No minimum period of service	5
Not sure	6

MQ45* Has the organizations' policy (view) on equal opportunities and the responsibilities of members of management been fully explained to you?

Yes   No
 1   2

MQ46* If your organization was to follow closely the provisions
of the equal opportunities policy (legislation), do you
believe that there would be significant changes in the
kinds of person recruited and promoted in the future?

Yes   No   Can't say
 1   2   3

MQ47 Since the introduction of the equal opportunities policy
(legislation), how much improvement has taken place
internally in the employment prospects of (1) women and
(2) black ethnic minority groups? (Please answer both
sections.)

(1) Prospects of women
   Significant improvement   1
   Some recognizable improvement   2
   No recognizable improvement   3
   Can't say   4

(2) Prospects of black ethnic minority groups
   Significant improvement   1
   Some recognizable improvement   2
   No recognizable improvement   3
   Can't say   4

MQ48 In your opinion, which of the following statements best
describes the attitude of internal trade union
representatives to the implementation of the equal
opportunity policy (legislation)? (Ring one answer only.)

Trade unions actively support the policy
(legislation)   1
Trade unions give some support to the policy
(legislation)   2
Trade unions show little interest in the policy
(legislation)   3
Trade unions are not committed to the objectives
of the policy (legislation)   4
Can't say   5

MQ49 Has the application of equal opportunities provisions
caused you any problems in your job?

Yes   No
 1   2

(question continued)

If *Yes*, please specify: ....

MQ50* How would you judge your own attitude to the aims of the equal opportunities policy (legislation)? (Ring one answer only.)

Fully support the aims of the equal opportunities policy (legislation)	1
On balance, support what the policy (legislation) is trying to achieve	2
Am not for or against the aims of the policy (legislation)	3
On balance do not support what the policy (legislation) is trying to achieve	4
Feel quite strongly against the aims of the equal opportunities policy (legislation)	5
Not sure	6

MQ51* In the last two years have you received any training (i.e. courses, seminars, briefing sessions) on the implications for recruitment and promotion of equal opportunities legislation and supporting codes of practice?

Yes   *No*
1   2

MQ52 What priority would you allocate to your training needs in relation to the equal opportunities policy and associated legislation?

High priority   *Medium priority*   *Low priority*   *No training needs*
1   2   3   4

MQ53 Please write here any further comments you wish to make on equality of opportunity within the organization.

Allow half a page for your answer.

Equal opportunity questions for employees

EQ1* In which department do you work?

Production	1
Engineering	2
Finance	3
Marketing	4
Research and development	5

EQ2   How would you describe your job?

Unskilled or semi-skilled   1
Skilled   2
Clerical/administrative   3
Technical   4

EQ3   What is your sex?

Male   1
Female   2

EQ4   To which one of the following racial groups do you belong?

Black Afro-Caribbean   1
Black Asian   2
Black British   3
White British   4
Other   5

Note: If you have ringed 'Other' please specify:

....

EQ5   Where is your job located?

Site A   1
Site B   2
Site C   3
Site D   4

EQ6   In your opinion, are there any jobs in your department which women could not carry out?

Yes   No
 1   2

If *Yes*, what are these jobs: ....

....

....

EQ7   In your opinion, are there any jobs in your department which men could not carry out?

Yes   No
 1   2

(question continued)

If *Yes*, what are these jobs: ....

....

....

EQ8* Do you believe that there are members of management/supervision in your department who consciously or subconsciously discriminate against women when recruiting or promoting?

Yes	*No*	*Can't say*
1	2	3

EQ9* In the last two years, has any man in your department been unfairly promoted ahead of a woman?

Yes	*No*	*No promotions in this period*	*Can't say*
1	2	3	4

EQ10 To what extent do you agree with the statement: 'Within the organization, a woman has an equal opportunity of achieving promotion to a senior management position as a man with similar ability'?

Agree	*Tend to agree*	*Not agree nor disagree*	*Tend to disagree*	*Disagree*
1	2	3	4	5

EQ11* To what extent do the following hinder the promotion of women to management positions within the organization? (Please answer all sections.)

	Is a definite hindrance	*Tends to be a hindrance*	*Is not a hindrance*
(1) Internal training opportunities available to women	1	2	3
(2) Qualifications required for management jobs, e.g. degree, HND, A levels	1	2	3
(3) Family commitments outside work	1	2	3

Note: If there are any other important hindrances not listed, please give details: ....

....

....

EQ12* In your opinion, are managers prepared to be more flexible in interpreting the requirements of jobs (e.g. qualifications, experience) when interviewing men than they are when interviewing women?

Yes   *No*   *Can't say*
1   2   3

EQ13 Are there any jobs in your department where (1) single and (2) married persons are preferred? (Please answer both sections.)

	Yes	No
(1) Jobs where single persons are preferred	1	2
(2) Jobs where married persons are preferred	1	2

If *Yes* to either (1) or (2), then please identify these jobs:

....

....

EQ14 In your job, do you work with any members of a black ethnic minority group?

Yes   *No*
1   2

EQ15 In the last two years has anyone been promoted ahead of a black person who, in your opinion, was better equipped for the vacant job?

Yes   *No*   *Can't say*
1   2   3

EQ16* Do you believe that there are members of management in your department who discriminate against members of black ethnic minority groups when recruiting or promoting?

Yes   *No*   *Can't say*
1   2   3

EQ17* To what extent do you agree with the statement: 'A member of a black ethnic minority group has an equal opportunity of obtaining employment with the organization as other applicants with similar ability'?

Agree	*Tend to agree*	*Not agree nor disagree*	*Tend to disagree*	*Disagree*
1	2	3	4	5

EQ18　In your opinion, do the following hinder black persons from getting jobs within your department? (Please answer all sections.)

	Yes	No	Not sure
(1) Job vacancies are not widely advertised	1	2	3
(2) Many jobs being filled by applicants recommended by current employees	1	2	3
(3) Lack of required qualifications/ experience	1	2	3
(4) Management bias in favour of white applicants	1	2	3

EQ19*　Do you believe that a black employee would be readily accepted by your workmates?

Yes	No	Can't say
1	2	3

EQ20*　Do you believe that a black supervisor would be readily accepted by your workmates?

Yes	No	Can't say
1	2	3

EQ21　To what extent do you agree with the following statements?

	Defin- itely agree	Tend to agree	Not agree nor disagree	Tend to disagree	Defin- itely disagree
(1) My ability is fully utilized in my present job	1	2	3	4	5
(2) I would like the opportunity to supervise other employees	1	2	3	4	5
(3) There are opportunities to get qualifications if I choose to do so	1	2	3	4	5
(4) I would refuse promotion if I had to move house	1	2	3	4	5
(5) There are opportunities for promotion in my job	1	2	3	4	5

(6) Within the organization, promotion is dependent upon an individuals' work performance   1   2   3   4   5

(7) Within the organization, women are encouraged to get on as much as men are   1   2   3   4   5

(8) The organization is good at identifying the right persons for promotion   1   2   3   4   5

EQ22 With respect to your department, to what extent do you agree/disagree with the following statements? (Please answer all sections.)

	Agree	Tend to agree	Not agree nor disagree	Tend to disagree	Dis-agree
(1) White applicants for jobs have no advantage over black applicants with similar ability	1	2	3	4	5
(2) In recruitment, job applicants with families are favoured over applicants who do not	1	2	3	4	5
(3) As a result of the Sex Discrimination Act for equal opportunities policy) all internal hindrances to women achieving senior management positions have been removed	1	2	3	4	5

(question continued)

	Agree	Tend to agree	Not agree nor disagree	Tend to disagree	Dis-agree
(4) Males employed on manual work would resist efforts of management to have women work alongside them	1	2	3	4	5
(5) Work groups comprised of all-white employees would resist management efforts to introduce black workers into these groups	1	2	3	4	5

EQ23   Has any member of management/supervision discussed with you the implications of the organization's equal opportunities policy?

Yes   No
1   2

EQ24*   If the organization was to follow closely the provisions of the equal opportunities policy (legislation) do you believe that there would be significant changes in the kinds of person recruited and promoted in the future?

Yes   No   Can't say
1   2   3

EQ25   Since the introduction of the equal opportunities policy (legislation), how much improvement has taken place in the employment prospects of (1) women and (2) black ethnic minority groups? (Please answer both sections.)

(1) Prospects of women
Significant improvement   1
Some recognizable improvement   2
Little/no recognizable improvement   3
Can't say   4

(2) Prospects of black ethnic minority groups
Significant improvement   1
Some recognizable improvement   2

Little/no recognizable improvement 3
Can't say 4

EQ26 In the last two years, has any workmate complained to you of having been unfairly treated on grounds of (1) race or (2) sex? (Please answer both sections.)

(1) Unfairly treated on grounds of race

Yes *No*
1 2

(2) Unfairly treated on grounds of sex

Yes *No*
1 2

EQ27 How would you judge your own attitude to the aims of the organization's equal opportunities policy (legislation)? (Ring one answer only.)

Fully support the aims of the equal
opportunities policy 1
On balance support what policy is
attempting to achieve 2
Am not for or against the aims of the policy 3
On balance do not support what the policy
is trying to achieve 4
Feel quite strongly against the aims of the
equal opportunities policy 5
Not sure 6

EQ28 Please write here any further comments you wish to make concerning the employment and career opportunities of women and members of ethnic minority groups.

Allow half a page for your answer.

Audit 4

Trade union representation and employee grievances

Introduction

This audit is obviously relevant to organizations employing trade union members. Non-unionized organizations with a staff association or other non-union system of employee representation may find that many of the questions can be modified to fit their own system of representation.

In unionized organizations many line managers will be expected to deal with issues raised by trade union representatives. Hence, they will need to be conversant with the internal policy on representation, i.e. accreditation of union representatives and the facilities afforded to them; role of personnel specialists; issues that are negotiable and those that are not; the function of IR committees; and the provisions of the grievance and other IR procedures.

Audits to date have shown that a majority of managers and supervisors in unionized organizations handle employee grievances and deal with trade union representatives. These audits have been very good at identifying those groups who have had the most involvement and have pinpointed many of the issues that have arisen as well as the problems encountered in dealing with them. Many important policy and training initiatives have been taken as a direct outcome of these audits.

An audit focusing upon this area of employee relations would normally be carried out with the intention of improving management performance in dealing with trade unions and handling grievances. Trade unions may view such an audit with some suspicion and their willing co-operation in the exercise may not be forthcoming. Consequently, only a management questionnaire is included in this section.

Audit objectives

These could be a selection of the following:

- to identify how often line managers deal with trade union representatives and the issues discussed;

- to assess the effectiveness of current IR policies and procedures;
- to identify areas where relationships with trade unions could be improved;
- to identify sources of employee grievances and problems encountered in resolving them;
- to identify areas where management performance in handling IR issues could be improved;
- to assess the respective roles of line managers and personnel specialists in grievances and other issues involving trade unions; and
- to identify management training needs.

Selection of participants

This is dealt with generally in Stage 2 (pages 8–10) in Part one. If your organization employs a significant number of technical experts who are graded as management but who supervise very few, or no, employees then this group might find many of the questions irrelevant to their jobs. In this situation you can either exclude them from completing a questionnaire or identify them by means of a question such as MQ3 and treat their answers differently to those of respondents supervising larger groups of employees.

Selection and modification of questions

Before attempting to write a questionnaire from the model questions, it is strongly recommended that you read very carefully the general guidelines outlined on pages (10–13) in Part one.

Variations of MQ1 and MQ2 have been used successfully many times in audits examining managers' involvement with trade unions and handling of grievances. If you wish to compare industrial relations in different sites then MQ4 can be used. If some of your managers and supervisors are trade union members then you might consider including MQ5. Clearly the responses of trade union members could differ from those of other line managers. However, you should be warned that the inclusion of MQ5 might generate suspicion and trade union opposition to the audit exercise.

The term 'trade union representative' has been used throughout the questions in this section. You might prefer to substitute shop steward, accredited representative or another term which is recognized in your organization.

Consider using training questions MQ19, MQ31, MQ32, and MQ47 even if you have not provided training in the past. When you formulate your recommendations it might be useful to demonstrate that little or no training has been provided to date.

Questions MQ21–MQ33 inclusive are only answered by respondents who have dealt with a trade union representative in the last twelve months. If you develop new questions on trade union representation you will have to decide whether you want all respondents to answer these questions or only those respondents who have dealt with representatives. This will clearly influence where the new questions are slotted into the question-naire. A similar decision will have to be made regarding new grievance questions as MQ41–MQ46 inclusive are only answered by those respondents who have handled grievances in the past twelve months.

MQ29 and MQ30 are questions requiring knowledge of the law. Although you might not consider these questions as relevant for your supervisors and middle managers, you could still include them in your questionnaire in order to discover whether your senior managers can answer them.

Analysing the information collected

General guidelines for summarizing the information from completed questionnaires and analysing the findings have been explained in Stages 6 and 7 in Part one (see pages 15–21).

You should begin your analysis by using the background informa-tion of respondents to compare the answers of different groups. For example, if you have asked a question to identify management grade then you can compare the responses of senior managers, middle managers, and supervisors for each question. Similarly, if you have asked a question to identify department then responses can be compared on this basis. Examples of things to look for in your analysis are as follows:

- Which management grades are most involved with trade union representatives?
- Are trade unions more active in some departments than others?
- How are relations with trade unions currently perceived by line managers?
- What is the level of understanding amongst managers of the internal IR policies and procedures?
- Is the grievance procedure understood by line managers and followed by them?
- What grievances and other issues are raised with line managers?
- Who has received training in the past and how effective has this been?
- How can additional training help to improve the current situation?

Past experience in this area indicates that an audit is likely to reveal a lot of information – especially on managers' involvement with trade union representatives – which was totally unexpected at the outset. Your audit will provide the information upon which you can formulate appropriate initiatives and direct them to those parts of your organization where they are most needed.

Questions for managers on trade union representation and employee grievances

MQ1* What is the grade of your job?

Grade 1 or 2	1
Grade 3-5	2
Grade 6 or above	3

MQ2* In which department do you work?

Production	1
Engineering	2
Finance	3
Marketing	4
Research and development	5

MQ3* How many employees report to you directly or indirectly via subordinate managers and supervisors?

5 or less	1
Between 6 and 25	2
26 or more	3

MQ4 Where is your job located?

Site A	1
Site B	2
Site C	3
Site D	4

MQ5 Are you a trade union member?

Yes   No
 1   2

MQ6 Which of the following statements best reflects the attitude of the organization with respect to trade union membership? (Ring one answer only.)

Employees are required to join a union as a condition of employment	1
Employees are encouraged to join a trade union but this is not a condition of employment	2
Union membership is neither encouraged nor discouraged	3
Non-membership is encouraged	4
Not sure	5

MQ7   In your area of responsibility, what proportion of employees are members of a trade union?

None	1
Up to 25%	2
26–50%	3
51–75%	4
Over 75%	5
Not sure	6

MQ8   In your area of responsibility, how has the proportion of unionized employees changed in the past two years?

Has increased	1
Has decreased	2
Is unchanged	3
Not sure	4

MQ9*   In your area of responsibility, which one of the following best describes the general attitude of employees to their trade union? (Ring one answer only.)

They are active trade unionists who seek an early union involvement in most issues that arise	1
They support their union and look to it to represent their interests in important issues	2
They are not very active trade unionists but sometimes approach their union when their own efforts to resolve issues are unsuccessful	3
They only approach their union in particularly exceptional circumstances	4
Can't say	5

MQ10*   In the last twelve months, have you encountered the resistance of trade unions to new methods of working in your area of responsibility?

Yes	*No*
1	2

MQ11   In the last twelve months, have employees in your area of responsibility taken any form of industrial action, e.g. go-slow, work-to-rule, overtime ban, strike?

Yes	*No*
1	2

MQ12* How would you evaluate the attitude of trade union representatives with regard to issues arising in your department? (Ring one answer only.)

Union reps show little interest in issues arising within the department	1
Union reps show an interest when important issues arise	2
Union reps demonstrate an interest in a range of issues	3
Reps are constantly on the look-out for issues to raise	4
Reps are very active and raise an unwarranted number of issues	5
Not in a position to comment	6

MQ13 How would you evaluate relations generally between management and trade unions within your department at present?

Relations are good	1
Relations are fairly good	2
Relations are reasonable	3
Relations tend to be strained	4
Relations are poor	5
Not in a position to comment	6

MQ14* Do you manage or supervise any employees who play an active role in a trade union (i.e. shop steward, committee member, branch official, safety representative)?

Yes	No	Not sure
1	2	3

MQ15* Are trade union representatives allowed *paid time off* from work for the following activities? (Please answer all questions.)

	Yes	No	Not sure
(1) Meetings with management	1	2	3
(2) Branch meetings with members	1	2	3
(3) TUC introductory course for shop stewards	1	2	3
(4) Off-site meetings with full-time union officers to discuss union business	1	2	3
(5) Representation of members at disciplinary interviews	1	2	3

MQ16* Does a union representative have the right to carry out the following activities *without first seeking permission of management?* (Please answer all sections.)

	Yes	No	Not sure
(1) Leave his/her job to attend a meeting of the joint consultative committee	1	2	3
(2) Use an internal telephone to call union headquarters in London	1	2	3
(3) Use notice boards to inform members of forthcoming branch meetings	1	2	3
(4) Invite a full-time union officer to attend a meeting on the site	1	2	3

MQ17* Have you received information on the range of facilities to be made available to representatives of a trade union (e.g. paid time off for TU duties, access to telephone and photocopying, training provisions)?

Yes	No	Not sure
1	2	3

MQ18 Are you personally expected to deal with trade union representatives with members working in your area of responsibility?

Yes	No	Not sure
1	2	3

MQ19* When did you last receive any off-the-job training (management seminars, briefings, courses, etc.) in *the internal policy on trade union representation* (i.e. recognition, union facilities, IR machinery, role of line managers, and personnel department)?

Within the last 2 years	1
From 2 to 5 years ago	2
Over 5 years ago	3
No off-the-job training received	4

MQ20* Over the last twelve months, how often on average have you had occasion to deal with trade union representatives acting on behalf of employees?

Daily	1
Weekly	2
Monthly	3
Occasionally	4
Never	5

Procedure: If the answer to MQ20 is 'Never' proceed to MQ34, otherwise proceed to MQ21.

MQ21* During the last twelve months, have you dealt with the following TU representatives? (Please answer all sections.)

	Yes	No
(1) Shop steward/staff representative	1	2
(2) Senior steward/convenor	1	2
(3) Branch official	1	2
(4) Full-time official employed by a trade union	1	2
(5) Safety representative	1	2
(6) Others not listed ·	1	2

MQ22* During the last twelve months, have your dealings with trade union representatives covered the items listed below? (Please answer all sections.)

	Yes	No
(1) Joint consultative matters	1	2
(2) Health and safety matters	1	2
(3) Disciplinary issues/cases	1	2
(4) Queries/grievances related to terms and conditions of employment	1	2
(5) Queries/grievances related to work/ departmental issues	1	2
(6) Introduction of changes in working methods/arrangements	1	2

Note: If you have had other dealings then please give details: ....
....
....

MQ23 During the last twelve months, has the frequency of your contacts with union representatives increased, decreased, or remained unchanged?

Increased	1
Decreased	2
Unchanged	3

MQ24 In an average week, how much time do you spend with trade union representatives who are acting on behalf of employees?

Under 1 hour	1
From 1 hour to half a day	2
Over half a day	3

MQ25* Which of the following describes most closely your dealings with trade union representatives? (N.B. In this context 'negotiation' is considered to involve bargaining between management and union representatives with a view to reaching *joint agreement.* 'Consultation' is considered to be seeking and taking into account the views of union representatives prior to *management taking decisions.*)

Negotiation	1
Mostly negotiation but some consultation	2
Equal negotiation and consultation	3
Mostly consultation but some negotiation	4
Consultation	5
None of the above	6

MQ26* During the last twelve months how often has there been a member of the personnel department *present* when you have dealt with trade union representatives?

Always	1
Most times	2
50% of the time	3
Occasionally	4
Never	5

MQ27 In the last twelve months, have you referred to the personnel department when dealing with an issue raised by a trade union representative?

Yes   No
1   2

MQ28 With regard to issues raised by trade union representatives in your department, how would you evaluate the current involvement of the personnel department? (Ring one answer only.)

The direct involvement of the personnel department should be decreased and departmental management given more authority to settle issues raised by trade unions	1
The personnel department should take a more active role in dealing with issues currently handled by departmental managers	2
The current involvement of the personnel department with respect to issues raised by trade unions should not be changed	3
Not in a position to comment	4

MQ29 According to law, can trade unions be denied certain information on the grounds that this might strengthen their negotiating position with management?

Yes   No   Not sure
1   2   3

MQ30 If a manager makes an agreement with a trade union that subcontracted work will only be carried out by trade union members, is the operation of such an agreement likely to be declared unlawful if it is challenged in a court of law?

Yes   No   Not sure
1   2   3

MQ31 When did the company last provide you with off-the-job training (management seminars, briefings, courses) which covered the legislation affecting trade unions, i.e. union membership, union activities, industrial action, facilities, disclosure of information?

Within the last two years   1
From 2 to 5 years ago   2
Over 5 years ago   3
No off-the-job training received 4

MQ32* When did the organization last provide you with off-the-job training (management, seminars, briefings, courses) which included negotiating skills?

Within the last two years   1
From 2 to 5 years ago   2
Over 5 years ago   3
No off-the-job training received 4

MQ33* Given the needs of your job, do you consider that (1) an update on the legislation affecting trade unions and (2) training in negotiating skills would be of benefit to you? (Please answer both sections.)

(1) Legislation affecting trade unions

Yes   No   Not sure
1   2   3

(2) Negotiating skills training

Yes   No   Not sure
1   2   3

MQ34* During the last twelve months, how often have the following been sources of employee grievances in your department? (N.B. A grievance is considered to be a complaint raised by one or more employees which if not resolved in the first instance could be pursued via a formal procedure.) (Please answer all sections.)

		Often	Occasion-ally	Seldom/never
(1)	Basic wages and salaries	1	2	3
(2)	Incentive bonus scheme	1	2	3
(3)	Workplace accommodation/facilities	1	2	3
(4)	Job evaluation/grading	1	2	3
(5)	Manning levels/workloads	1	2	3
(6)	Work methods/job content	1	2	3
(7)	Promotion/temporary promotion	1	2	3
(8)	Overtime working	1	2	3
(9)	Subcontracted work	1	2	3
(10)	Holidays	1	2	3
(11)	Maternity provisions	1	2	3
(12)	Actions of management/supervision	1	2	3

MQ35 When raising a grievance with management, has the employee concerned an *automatic entitlement* to be accompanied by a union representative or colleague?

Yes   No   Not sure
  1   2   3

MQ36* If an employee has a grievance, how should this be raised with management *in the first instance*?

Employees should raise it *personally*
with the immediate supervisor   1
Employee and his/her union rep. should raise
it *together* with the immediate supervisor   2
The union rep. should raise it *alone* with
the immediate supervisor   3
Not sure   4

MQ37 Can a manager or supervisor refuse to process an employee complaint via the grievance procedure if he/she considers that the complaint has no reasonable grounds?

Yes   No   Not sure
  1   2   3

MQ38   Do you possess an up-to-date copy of the grievance
procedure?

Yes   *No*   *Not sure*
  1   2   3

MQ39*   Have the steps in the grievance procedure and your role
in it, been explained to you?

Yes   *No*   *Not sure*
  1   2   3

MQ40*   During the last twelve months, how often on average
have you had occasion to deal with employee grievances?

Daily	1
Weekly	2
Monthly	3
Occasionally	4
Never	5

Procedure: If the answer to MQ40 is 'Never' proceed to MQ47,
otherwise proceed to MQ41.

MQ41   During the last twelve months, how many times have you
used the grievance procedure to deal with issues raised
by employees?

Never   *Once or*   *Three or*
          twice   *more times*
  1   2   3

MQ42   How would you assess the impact of the grievance
procedure upon the way in which employee grievances
are handled by members of management?

Procedure is of assistance	1
Procedure is a hindrance	2
Procedure has little relevance	3
Can't say	4

MQ43*   Are you clear about the limits of your authority when
dealing with employee grievances, i.e. issues that can be
settled by yourself and those which should be referred to
more senior management or to the personnel
department?

Yes   *No*
  1   2

MQ44* How often do employees in your department take their grievances to a trade union representative before raising them personally with a member of management?

Always   1
Usually   2
50% of the time   3
Occasionally   4
Never   5

MQ45 During the past twelve months, have you sought the advice or assistance of the personnel department over a grievance raised with you by an employee or union representative?

Yes   No
1   2

MQ46* During the last twelve months, how often have the following caused you problems in the handling of employee grievances? (Please answer all sections.)

		Often	*Occasion-ally*	*Seldom/ never*
(1)	Lack of information available to resolve grievance	1	2	3
(2)	Insufficient authority to settle at your level of management	1	2	3
(3)	Reluctance of other managers, supervisors, etc., to handle issues	1	2	3
(4)	Unreasonable attitudes of employees/trade union reps	1	2	3
(5)	Lack of support from personnel department	1	2	3

Note: If there have been other sources of problems not listed above, then please give details:

....

....

....

MQ47* When did you last receive off-the-job training in the handling of employee grievances which was provided by the organization?

Within the last 2 years   1
From 2 to 5 years ago   2

(question continued)

Over 5 years ago   3
No training received   4

MQ48* Given the needs of your job, do you consider that training in the handling of employee grievances would be of benefit to you?

Yes	*No*	*Not sure*
1	2	3

MQ49* Please write here any further comments you wish to make concerning trade union representation and the handling of grievances.

Allow half a page for your answer.

Audit 5

Disciplinary matters

Introduction

Managers and supervisors with responsibility for employees are normally required to ensure that acceptable standards of work performance and behaviour are achieved. When employees fail to meet the required standards, then the manager or supervisor is expected to take action. This could involve counselling, an informal 'telling off' or, for more serious offences, the initiation of a stage in the disciplinary procedure.

Experience to date has shown that personnel departments and senior line managers frequently underestimate the frequency with which disciplinary offences occur and the extent to which line managers take disciplinary action. Audits have proven a useful tool for determining the actual situation. They have also revealed inadequacies in the disciplinary procedure and highlighted training needs.

As the handling of disciplinary matters is primarily a management responsibility and most employees are unlikely to have had first-hand experience of disciplinary situations, only a management questionnaire is perceived as appropriate. Consequently, there are no employee questions included in this section.

Audit objectives

If line managers are to be asked to supply information which accurately reflects the current situation in this sensitive area, then it is recommended that the stated objectives should not be perceived as threatening to them. Acceptable objectives could be as follows:

- to determine current practices for handling disciplinary matters;
- to identify areas of the organization where there is scope for improving standards of work performance and behaviour;
- to assess the current operation of the disciplinary procedure;
- to review the respective roles of line managers and personnel specialists in disciplinary matters;

- to evaluate the current level of understanding of the disciplinary procedure and unfair dismissal legislation;
- to evaluate the effectiveness of current management training in disciplinary matters; and
- to identify the training needs of managers and supervisors in the handling of disciplinary matters.

Selection of participants

This is dealt with generally in Stage 2 (pages 8–10) of Part one. Disciplinary matters are of direct relevance to those who supervise or manage employees. For this reason some organizations have chosen to limit participation to those managers and supervisors responsible for five or more employees. An alternative criteria for determining participation could be to include all managers and supervisors with a role in disciplinary procedures.

Selection and modification of questions

Before attempting to write a questionnaire from the model questions it is strongly recommended that you read very carefully the general guidelines outlined on pages (10–13) in Part one.

When considering the background information questions, i.e. MQ1–MQ5, respondents should be asked to supply no more than three or four pieces of information about themselves and their jobs, otherwise fears about confidentiality are likely to arise. With respect to disciplinary matters, it is important to identify the managerial level of respondents as this is likely to be related to their authority to initiate action and their role in the disciplinary procedure. Hence, it is strongly recommended that MQ1 should be retained and modified in the light of your own management grading system. You will need to be able to differentiate between the responses of supervisors, middle managers, and senior managers when considering your findings. Also department (or function) has proven to be a key variable in identifying differences in line managers' involvement in disciplinary matters and it is suggested that a suitably modified version of MQ2 should be retained.

Several questions refer to behaviour (conduct), e.g. MQ7 and MQ13, if you select these questions use *either* behaviour *or* conduct in your wording.

There are quite a number of questions referring to standards of work performance and behaviour; avoid duplication by being selective in those you retain.

If MQ14 is to be used then 'staff and manual employees' should be modified to suit your own internal language, e.g. 'monthly and weekly paid employees', 'office and works staff'.

MQ17 and MQ19 seek similar information, hence, do not retain both.

If you have different disciplinary procedures for staff and white-collar employees then you will have to specify which procedure you are referring to in MQ16, MQ17, and MQ18.

For MQ20, MQ23, MQ36, and MQ37 you should consult your disciplinary procedure(s) and amend these questions accordingly.

If you develop additional questions consider where they best fit in the questionnaire. If you want all respondents to answer these new questions include them *before* MQ26. If you want them answered only by respondents who have set in motion disciplinary action, then place them *after* MQ26.

If supervisors and middle managers are not expected to be conversant with unfair dismissal legislation do not automatically reject questions such as MQ25 and MQ39. You could include these questions but only analyse the answers of senior managers.

If your managers have received no training to date, and one of your objectives is to identify training needs, do not automatically reject MQ41. It might be useful to have statistics which clearly demonstrate that training to date has been non-existent.

Analysing the information collected

General guidelines for summarizing the information from completed questionnaires and analysing the findings are included in stages 6 and 7 of Part one (see pages 15–21).

You should begin your analysis by using the grade, department, or site of respondents to compare the answers of particular groups. Bearing in mind your audit objectives and the questions you decided to use, begin your analysis by establishing:

- Are there any sites or departments whose disciplinary standards are a particular problem?
- What disciplinary offences occur most frequently?
- How well do managers and supervisors understand their roles and responsibilities in disciplinary matters?
- Are disciplinary rules being applied consistently across the organization?
- Are the provisions of the disciplinary procedure being followed?
- Are the current levels of authority to initiate disciplinary sanctions satisfactory?
- How effective is the role of the personnel department in disciplinary matters?
- Who has received training and how effective has this been?
- What existing training needs exist?

After your initial analysis has been completed you may choose to carry out further analysis with respect to particularly interesting findings. For example, you could identify those managers and supervisors who have been involved with the suspension or dismissal of an employee and examine their level of understanding of the disciplinary procedure and the law. It might prove useful to you to compare the answers of particular sub-groups such as:

(a) those who have received training and those who have not;
(b) those who have contacted the personnel department and those who have not; and
(c) those who possess a copy of the disciplinary procedures and those who do not.

Once your analysis has been completed you will have a very good picture of the current situation and be in a position to select appropriate initiatives to tackle any deficiencies that have been revealed.

Discipline questions for managers

MQ1*   What is your management grade?

Grade 1 or 2   1
Grade 3–5   2
Grade 6 or above   3

MQ2*   In which department do you work?

Production   1
Maintenance   2
Finance   3
Research and development   4

MQ3*   What is the total number of employees reporting to you
         directly or indirectly via subordinate managers or
         supervisors?

5 or less   1
6–15   2
16–25   3
More than 25   4

MQ4*   Where is your job location?

Site A   1
Site B   2
Site C   3
Site D   4

MQ5*   What is your age group?

30 and under   1
31–50   2
51 and over   3

MQ6*   Are there any employees in your area of responsibility
         whose level of performance in their job frequently falls
         below a standard acceptable to you?

Yes   *No*
1   2

MQ7*   Are there any employees in your area of responsibility
         whose behaviour (conduct) frequently falls below a
         standard acceptable to you?

Yes   *No*
1   2

MQ8   To what extent do you record (1) lateness and (2) absenteeism in your area of responsibility? (Please answer both sections.)

(1) Lateness
Record all lateness   1
Only record lateness of
persistent offenders   2
Do not record lateness   3

(2) Absenteeism
Record all absenteeism   1
Only record absenteeism of
persistent offenders   2
Do not record absenteeism   3

MQ9   In your department, are there managers and supervisors who 'turn a blind eye' towards employees whose work performance or behaviour frequently falls below an acceptable level?

Yes   No   Can't say
1   2   3

MQ10   Are there any managers/supervisors in your department whose own work performance and/or behaviour is so unsatisfactory that it has a detrimental effect upon the disciplinary standards of employees?

Yes   No   Can't say
1   2   3

MQ11   In your department, are there any identifiable patterns of absenteeism amongst certain work groups?

Yes   No   Can't say
1   2   3

MQ12*   With respect to employees in your department, to what extent do you believe it is possible to achieve (1) improvements in work performance, (2) reductions in absenteeism, and (3) reductions in lateness? (Please answer all sections.)

(1) Work performance
Could be improved a great deal   1
Could be improved significantly   2
There is some scope for improvement   3
Little/no improvement is possible   4
Can't say   5

(2) Absenteeism

Could be reduced a great deal	1
Could be reduced significantly	2
There is some scope for a reduction	3
Little/no reduction is possible	4
Can't say	5

(3) Lateness

Could be reduced a great deal	1
Could be reduced significantly	2
There is some scope for a reduction	3
Little/no reduction is possible	4
Can't say	5

MQ13 In your opinion, how successful is your department in achieving high standards of (1) work performance and (2) behaviour (conduct) from employees? (Please answer both sections.)

(1) Standards of work performance

High standards are consistently achieved	1
Fairly good overall standards are achieved	2
Standards are acceptable	3
Difficulty is encountered in maintaining acceptable standards	4
Standards overall are not acceptable	5

(2) Standards of behaviour (conduct)

High standards are consistently achieved	1
Fairly good overall standards are achieved	2
Standards are acceptable	3
Difficulty is encountered in maintaining acceptable standards	4
Standards overall are not acceptable	5

MQ14 In your opinion are different standards applied to staff and manual employees with respect to lateness and absenteeism?

Yes	No	Can't say
1	2	3

MQ15 Are there significant differences between departments in the standards of (1) work performance and (2) behaviour (conduct), required of employees? (Please answer both sections.)

(question continued)

(1) Required standards of work performance
There are significant differences
between departments   1
There are no significant differences
between departments   2
Can't say   3

(2) Required standards of behaviour (conduct)
There are significant differences
between departments   1
There are no significant differences
between departments   2
Can't say   3

MQ16* Do you possess, or have ready access to, an up-to-date
copy of the disciplinary procedure?

Possess a copy   1
Ready access to a copy   2
No ready access to a copy   3

MQ17* Do you have a role in the disciplinary procedure?

Yes   No   Not sure
 1   2   3

MQ18 Do trade union representatives have a role in the
disciplinary procedure?

Yes   No   Not sure
 1   2   3

MQ19 Is it part of your job to initiate disciplinary action, i.e.
issue verbal warnings or take more serious disciplinary
actions?

Yes   No   Not sure
 1   2   3

MQ20* Have you the personal authority to initiate the following
disciplinary actions *without prior reference to senior
management or personnel/IR? (Please answer all sections.)*

	Yes	*No*	*Not sure*
(1) Issue verbal warnings	1	2	3
(2) Issue written warnings	1	2	3
(3) Suspend without pay	1	2	3
(4) Dismiss	1	2	3

MQ21* Are your responsibilities clearly defined in your department with regard to disciplinary matters, i.e. the stages at
which you should become involved and the extent of
your authority?

Yes   *No*   *Not sure*

1   2   3

MQ22 Whilst initiating formal disciplinary action against an
employee, is it *necessary* to inform the employee
concerned that he/she is entitled to be represented
during the disciplinary interview by a union
representative or colleague?

Yes   *No*   *Not sure*

1   2   3

MQ23 If a manager or supervisor takes formal disciplinary action
against an employee, after what period of time does the
employee lose the right of appeal? (Ring one answer
only.)

Must lodge appeal at time of disciplinary interview	1
Must appeal within 5 working days	2
Must appeal within 10 working days	3
Must appeal within four weeks	4
Employees are not entitled to appeal	5
Not sure	6

MQ24* In a case involving gross misconduct, how many warnings
is the employee concerned entitled to have before he/she
can be dismissed?

Two warnings	1
One warning	2
No warnings	3
Not sure	4

MQ25* If a new recruit successfully completes a trial period of
employment, according to law can management
subsequently dismiss him/her fairly on the grounds of
unsatisfactory work performance if this deteriorates at a
later date?

Yes   *No*   *Not sure*

1   2   3

MQ26* During the last two years, approximately how many times have you set in motion disciplinary action against an employee?

(N.B. This includes the issuing of a verbal warning as well as more serious sanctions.)

Never	1
Once or twice	2
Three to five times	3
More than five times	4

Procedure: If the answer to MQ26 is 'Never', proceed to MQ40, otherwise proceed to MQ27.

MQ27* In the disciplinary cases in which you have been involved in the last two years, have the following disciplinary sanctions been imposed? (Please answer all sections.)

	Yes	*No*
(1) Verbal warning	1	2
(2) Written warning	1	2
(3) Suspension with pay	1	2
(4) Suspension without pay	1	2
(5) Dismissal	1	2
(6) Other action, please give details		

....

MQ28 In the disciplinary cases *personally handled by you* in the last two years, were the following steps always carried out? (Please answer all sections.)

	Yes	*No*	*Not personally handled any cases*
(1) The personal file always checked for previous disciplinary offences	1	2	3
(2) A structured method for conducting the interviews always followed	1	2	3
(3) The employee always advised of his/her right of appeal	1	2	3

MQ29* Have you fully recorded details of all disciplinary cases you have personally handled during the last two years, i.e. details of dates, times, incidents, explanations received, action taken?

Yes	No	Not personally handled any cases
1	2	3

MQ30 During the last two years, have you contacted the personnel/IR department over a disciplinary case?

Yes No
1 2

Procedure: If the answer to MQ30 is Yes, proceed to MQ31, otherwise proceed to MQ32.

MQ31 During the last two years, have you contacted the personnel/IR department concerning a disciplinary case for the following reasons? (Please answer all sections.)

	Yes	No
(1) To inform personnel/IR of action taken	1	2
(2) For advice on rules/procedures	1	2
(3) For advice on legislation	1	2
(4) For assistance in carrying out disciplinary action	1	2
(5) For action to be taken by personnel/ IR specialist	1	2

MQ32* With regard to disciplinary matters arising in your department, should the role of the personnel department be increased or decreased? (Ring one answer only.)

The involvement of the personnel department should be decreased and departmental management given more authority to deal with disciplinary matters	1
The personnel department should take a more active role in disciplinary matters currently handled by departmental management	2
The current involvement of the personnel department in disciplinary matters should not be changed	3
Not in a position to comment	4

MQ33* In your opinion, does the disciplinary procedure set the authority (1) to issue a written warning and (2) to dismiss, at a level of management which is too high or too low?

(1) To issue a written warning	
Authority is set too high	1
Authority is set too low	2
Authority is about right	3
Not in a position to comment	4

(question continued)

115

(2) To dismiss
Authority is set too high   1
Authority is set too low   2
Authority is about right   3
Not in a position to comment   4

MQ34   In your opinion, is the disciplinary procedure of assistance, or a hindrance, to the effective handling of disciplinary matters by line managers?

Procedure is of assistance to line managers   1
Procedure is a hindrance to line managers   2
I am not in a position to comment   3

MQ35*   In those disciplinary cases with which you have had an involvement in the last two years, have the following factors been a source of problem to you? (Please answer all sections.)

	Yes	No
(1) Failure of other managers/supervisors to comply with the requirements of the disciplinary procedure	1	2
(2) Inadequate records of past offences	1	2
(3) Inadequate guidance material on rules, procedures, and sanctions	1	2
(4) Inadequate support from more senior managers	1	2
(5) Inadequate support from personnel/ IR department	1	2
(6) Inadequate personal authority to initiate suitable action	1	2

MQ36   What is the maximum period of time that members of management should keep a record of a formal verbal warning in the personal file of the employee concerned? (Ring one answer only.)

Record in file for 6 months   1
Record in file for 12 months   2
Record in file for 2 years   3
Record in file permanently   4
Record in file only for duration
of improvement period   5
Period at manager's discretion   6
Not sure   7

MQ37   For what period of time does a written warning remain valid? (Ring one answer only.)

6 months	1
12 months	2
Permanently	3
Period at manager's discretion	4
Only for duration of improvement period	5
Not sure	6

MQ38   Does the internal disciplinary procedure require members of management to take any additional measures when formally disciplining a union representative to those normally taken when disciplining other employees?

Yes   No   Not sure
1   2   3

MQ39   In the event of an employee being dismissed for unsatisfactory work performance, what is the legal minimum length of service the employee must have completed before he/she is entitled to process a claim for unfair dismissal at an industrial tribunal? (Ring one answer only.)

Must have 13 weeks service	1
Must have 26 weeks service	2
Must have one year's service	3
Must have two years' service	4
There is no legal minimum service	5
Not sure	6

MQ40*   With respect to disciplinary matters, how would you evaluate the levels of knowledge of trade union representatives and members of management?

Union representatives are generally more knowledgeable	1
Members of management are generally more knowledgeable	2
There is little or no difference	3
Not in a position to comment	4

MQ41*   When did the organization last provide you with off-the-job training (management seminars, briefings, courses, etc.), in the handling of disciplinary matters?

Within the last 2 years	1
From 2 to 5 years ago	2
Over 5 years ago	3
No off-the-job training received	4

MQ42* How would you evaluate the training you have received in disciplinary matters?

Comprehensive training received	1
Training received covering the most important aspects	2
Some training received but certain important aspects not covered	3
No training received	4

MQ43* Do you consider that your training in the handling of disciplinary matters needs updating?

Yes	No	Not sure
1	2	3

MQ44* Please write here any further comments you wish to make on disciplinary matters within the organization.

Allow half a page for your answer.

Index

For Product Safety Concerns and Information please contact our EU
representative GPSR@taylorandfrancis.com Taylor & Francis Verlag GmbH,
Kaufingerstraße 24, 80331 München, Germany

Printed and bound by CPI Group (UK) Ltd, Croydon, CR0 4YY
08/05/2025
01864461-0001